LIVING AN AWAKENED LIFE

THE LESSONS OF LOVE

This edition published by
Synchronicity Foundation International.
2610 Adial Rd., Faber, VA 22938 USA
with Tandava Press

ISBN 10: 1-884068-01-4
ISBN 13: 978-1-884068-01-0 First Edition

Cover Design by Sumit Shringi

Living an Awakened Life: The Lessons of Love
by Master Charles Cannon with Will Wilkinson

Reference: 1. Spirituality. 2. Master Charles Cannon.
3. Synchronicity Foundation, Inc. 4. Self-Help Techniques.

DEDICATION

This book is dedicated to every questing individual who knows in their heart that there is more to life than survival.

Regardless of your beliefs, your status in life, your confidence or doubts, life has guided you here to these pages, which means that you are ready to take this step in your evolving, human experience, to become that "more" you have been seeking.

May you find inspiration and comfort in these lessons in love that follow, so you can live a truly awakened life.

৵

CONTENTS

ACKNOWLEDGMENTS

Every book takes a team to grow ideas into printed form. Thank you to all who assisted in this process. Thank you, also, to those researchers and writers who have toiled to provide the statistics and commentary we have referenced throughout the chapters.

Looking forward, we acknowledge all those who will find personal value in these weekly lessons in love and apply what's learned. Our grandchildren will be depending on you for leadership in a future world of complexity that we cannot imagine today. Today is for choosing to live an awakened life.

&

INTRODUCTION

Welcome to a unique reading adventure.

What follows is a series of 52 explorations, providing a focus of inspiration and motivation, week-by-week throughout the year.

Each presentation is dated so that you can start today, whatever the day is. We recommend reading it once or twice during each week and using a journal to track your progress on the various themes of spiritual awakening and holistic awareness.

The book is segmented into the four seasons, framed by solstice and equinox, which are particularly significant pivot dates in the annual calendar. You'll notice that individual presentations blend with each other and repetition is employed deliberately in order to emphasize vital points and help you sift emerging understanding deeper into your own, personal database.

You're about to discover a fundamentally different definition and articulation of love. True love is more than emotion, more than romance. It is the truth of who you innately are. Love is another word for God, for source intelligence, for consciousness, for whatever you name the truth of life in the universe. Love is the language of this book.

This book is also a manual for growing your wakeful experience into a full-time reality, sustained with ease regardless of day-to-day challenges. Each chapter follows a four-part formula, beginning with an invitation to stretch your imagination muscles with a question: *"What if...?"* This is followed by an insight drawn from the material, then an action to undertake, and finally a personal quality to celebrate.

This formula is designed to help you integrate what you are reading incrementally so that, week by week, you continue diving deeper into the understanding of what it means to live an awakened life with a focus on love.

Thank you for your commitment to conscious evolution and your willingness to undertake this journey and become an example for others who yearn for the same fulfillment. With the benefit of these weekly empowerments you can provide a valuable contribution and inspiration to family, friends, community, and the world at large.

&

PART ONE

WELCOME TO WINTER

WELCOME TO WINTER

"Winter is the time for comfort, for good food and warmth,
for the touch of a friendly hand
and for a talk beside the fire:
it is the time for home."[1]
- Edith Sitwell

Winter is a time of gestation, meditation, contemplation, looking into yourself. While the natural world sleeps, we can drop deeper into source, embracing the causative level of our experience, contemplating what is real and true, and we can open to ever-expanding possibilities within ourselves.

The seed of your true nature is here, awaiting you. Winter is the season to explore the interior of your being, to trust that the seed of love you are will spring to life. You are getting in touch with the truth of who you are.

You are invited by the turning tide of life to change paradigms, to update your database, to recognize the nature of illusion and truth. This can bring you into a greater understanding of relative reality—the one is the many, the many are one—and the process of illusory dominant enculturation that we all consider to be the only "reality."

Winter bids us welcome another possibility, while acknowledging this one fully. We have been having the experience of *what we are not*. That can be a blessing, if it leads us to awaken to the experience of *what we are*.

In winter, we sleep. We ready ourselves to further awaken to the revelation that we have been mired in illusion... and that we have also glimpsed the truth. We sense a new season coming, a time for building truth. This is the basis of all wisdom traditions—to develop the dominance of truth, reversing our experience from fear to love.

Meditation is the foremost technique for culturing this changing of the seasons. Those quiet moments within bring balance, an increasing balance that expands awareness, that beckons our awakening, then builds the rising of all-embracing love over the cloying grip of fear.

Winter heralds the coming triumph of truth over illusion. Let us embrace the tradition of meditation, in its many forms, as a sacred container for our inner process of transformation.

Winter is a time for self-love, to be a willing student of life who comes to know that love must first dawn within us (love for ourselves) before we can experience the truth of love with any other.

It's all here in the dark: an abused childhood; growing up with demons; being shamed for our bodies and for not living up to our potential in work and in life; and memories of failures and dashed dreams.

We are not alone in our self-negation. Everyone has their own unique issues around self-worth, self-acceptance, self-love. Our first step into freedom is to rise above that quagmire into the causative level of love. Can you love the life that empowers you, the experience of life without which you have nothing? You are alive! Loving *this*, the experience of life itself makes it possible to open to source.

This is what it means to love yourself. You learn the truth, that love is your very nature. You open to the loving energy that already empowers you, that which you already are. Once you are resonating with that, illusions of self-worth begin to crumble, just as the winter snow melts in spring.

You will be looking at life through a different lens, through the eyes of love.

Socrates said that 99% of what we believe is not true. Open now to what *is* true: you are already *it*, you are what you have been seeking, you *are* the love you have longed for. And here, in the quiet of winter, you effortlessly shift into a Zen perspective: *just this, just this, this is it.*

"What you are looking for is what is looking."[2]
- St Francis of Assisi

Chapter One, December 21 WINTER

THE FUTURE OF LOVE

*"Pain and illness, the deaths of those one loves,
and discomforts and disappointments mar the
happy norm, but they do not alter the fact that
happiness is the norm."[1]*
- Jean Liedloff

Recall a sunny winter day in childhood by a stream in the woods, revel in the memory of an afternoon of soaring intimacy, hear again the kind words of a friend consoling you on a wrenching loss. These are encounters with love, more than emotion or attraction or desire. This is communion, sacred, more than just memories, threshold marks on your evolving soul.

Regardless of the details, your senses engaged in remarkable ways. In her essay, "The Skill of Ecological Perception," Harvard lecturer Laura Sewall writes, *"Skillful perception is the practice of intentionally sensing with our eyes, pores, and hearts wide open. It requires receptivity and the participation of our whole selves, despite the potential pain. ... It is allowing one's identity and boundaries to be permeable and flexible."[2]*

This sentiment is echoed in a traditional Native American prayer: *"Give us the wisdom to teach our children to love, to respect and be kind to one another, so that we may grow with peace in mind."[3]* Learning to love is the answer that has eluded us. This is what develops peace in the mind, which leads to a fundamentally different attitude towards the earth.

American philosopher David Abram wrote, *"The ecological crisis may be the result of a recent and collective perceptual disorder in our species, a unique form of myopia which it now forces us to correct."[4]*

Time will soon tell if enough of us can make this correction and, looking through the eyes of love, find novel ways to care for our home planet and each other and—miraculously—collaborate towards survival as a species. Perhaps we might even begin a new and more noble chapter in our human story.

It would begin with respect for life. The era of arrogant human exceptionalism, which has swelled to perhaps terminal narcissism, would give way to humble brotherhood, acknowledging the community of life we inhabit. That community thrives on the currency of love and there is no shortage of love, no poverty and no hoarding.

For those of us uncomfortable with love, it's a challenge to open and receive what we want so desperately yet shrink from throughout years of disempowerment. "I am not enough" is the secret mantra so many people endure every day. But love is unconditional and we can come to the party exactly as we are.

In fact, that's a clue about love's true nature: it's accepting and inclusive. Hence the madness of judgment in the name of love. God loves indiscriminately and one of his most courageous prophets said something like "whatever you did for one of the least of these brothers and sisters of mine, you did for me." That's worth remembering the next time we withhold our love from someone we've judged unworthy. That's always a self-judgment, by the way, and the best way to release that is to love unconditionally.

What if love is your core essence?

INSIGHT
True wisdom is self-love.
I am love and therefore I can be loving.

ACTION
Stand before a mirror and say: "I love you."
Notice what arises in thoughts and feelings.

Celebrate the truth of who you are
and what you are becoming.

LOOKING THROUGH THE EYES OF LOVE

"It is difficult to get the news from poems
yet men die miserably every day
for lack of what is found there."[1]
– William Carlos Williams

Looking through the eyes of love changes everything: we see the world anew. As Czech philosopher and writer Erazim Kohak wrote, *"Set aside the learned ways of perceiving the world as dead matter for your use and see if you can recover again your actual perception of the world as a community of beings to whom you are meaningfully related."[2]* This experience requires perception through the "heart-field" and it affords us an expanded sense of self, connected with each other and life forms of all kinds.

Perception through the heart is profoundly different. Diversity is honored as complementary, and uniqueness is the cherished norm. Heart intelligence equips us to live with grace in the world of a million things, celebrating how they all fit together, not demanding they unify into a simplistic order for easier control.

Past President of Earth Island Institute, Carl Anthony, wrote, *"People who believe, as I do, that the ecological threat is real, believe we have to construct a self capable of harboring the voices of many different people and cultures, not just so–called white people. This is what I mean by a genuinely multi-cultural self. The truth of the matter is: we have an official story about who we are as a people, who is really important, who's in the mainstream and who isn't. This story is like refined sugar. It's not a real story about real people. It's been packaged and processed beyond recognition. I don't believe it includes stories of most people in this country; but in particular history is deficient for dealing with the reality of people of color."[3]*

The very notion of "people of color," exposes our fragmented thinking. When I think of God, the primary quality that arises in my awareness relates to oneness, not separation. Racism takes many forms and targets many distinctions but it always sits on a conceptual throne of exceptionalism. Thus, the conceptual separation between God and humans reflects as separation between types of humans. There seems to be little reason to champion a remedy that increases separation by propelling humans on a course of duplication and replacement. Who needs God... who needs to merge with God, if we can be that on our own?

Instead, we meet in love, unified not by compromise but in the oneness that transcends all divisiveness, the oneness that we already are. This cannot be known in theory. It's a full-body, full-hearted experience of communion beyond differences, the embrace that no judgment can thwart, compassion without conditions, and forgiveness that requires nothing of the other. Such love is fulfillment and, once savored, leads us on, deeper into the feast, where we eat with our hearts and digest with our souls, and are transformed by love into the truth of what we've always been: love.

What if the love you are encompasses all beings?

INSIGHT
True wisdom is experiencing that the many are the one and the one is the many.
I am one with all.

ACTION
Walking down the street and noticing how different we all are.
Then noticing how we are all the same.

Celebrate your oneness with all and love yourself as all.

Chapter Three, January 4   WINTER

FLOWING LOVE

"If we could somehow master the technology of being in the right place at the right time, if we could learn to ride the flow of synchronicity, then we would have accessed a power greater than anything the world of force is capable of."[1]
- Charles Eisenstein

Human experience has been polarized in the negative. For many who are awakening to this suffocating dysfunction, dominance is now reversing towards the positive. This realigns our emotional expression from fear to love. The implications are profound.

If we survive the plethora of environmental threats, our continuing evolution will eventually produce Humanity 2.0, characterized by a fundamental inclusiveness. This begins with a deepening connection with cosmic consciousness as well as with the natural world.

Connection goes in both directions, which turns out to be one direction. Even to say that we sit in the middle implies disconnection. Whatever "God" might be to each of us (and whatever we imagine our humanness to be) is all the same "thing," a no-thing, mostly space. Our awareness of this is expanding, inevitably, to the degree we are open to it, and the actual experience of increasing connection is the 21st century hallmark of conscious evolution.

Futurist Ray Kurzweil wrote: *"So as we evolve, we become closer to God. Evolution is a spiritual process. There is beauty and love and creativity and intelligence in the world — it all comes from the neocortex. So we're going to expand the brain's neocortex and become more Godlike."[2]*

There's probably more involved than expanding the brain's neo-cortex. When Kurzweil peers into the future, he sees the wonders that technology may provide. When I peer into the future, I see a world filled with more and more individuals sharing a spirit/nature-based experience of oneness, and I feel hopeful. I welcome what is coming, sensing that what's developing is some kind of unimaginable merger between native and technological intelligence and that the offspring of this marriage will be something entirely new — Humanity 2.0.

What that will be, exactly, must remain a mystery until it fully manifests; yet somewhere within me, I know that *this* is the future of love. Dystopian nightmares of dark futures with enslaved humans reflect our worst dreams. What of the light? What of a bright future where love conquers fear, where cooperation replaces competition, a world where we all belong? This is what we are evolving towards, focusing our attention on "being the change we wish to see in the world" by expanding our awareness and our embrace, to welcome all that we have dismissed as less than us or too different from us or threatening to our guarded place in the world.

Throw open the gates! True security needs no unnatural borders, nothing kept separate (including ourselves) from the one that we already are. This is the future of love and love is the path we travel to get there.

What if a new chapter in human experience is dawning?

INSIGHT
*Walking down the street and noticing
how different we all are.
Then notice how we are all the same.*

ACTION
*Open to the possibility of
unimaginable personal transformation.
Notice what thoughts and feelings arise.*

Celebrate your choice to be born into this possibility.

Chapter Four, January 11   WINTER

THE MARRIAGE OF BIOLOGY AND TECHNOLOGY

"What we send out comes back to us
in the same frequency but amplified.
If we send out positive, thankful vibrations,
positive vibrations will return.
If we send out negative vibrations,
negative vibrations and experiences will return.
What goes around, comes around, as the old saying goes."[1]
- David Banner

The Beach Boys sang about "Good Vibrations;" it was one of their most popular songs. *"Gotta keep those lovin', good vibrations a'happenin' with you."[2]* Many of us can still sing along with that tune; it has an emotional appeal that has endured for decades. Why? Perhaps because we recognize that it is inherently true.

The song may have even awakened some kind of primal understanding in us. What I've termed "the awakening impulse" comes in many forms. Its purpose is to increase the experience of love. It has no interest in improving an imbalanced status quo or improving the chances for human survival at a stagnating level of fragmented consciousness. The priority—happening everywhere except where we humans fight it—is to continue expanding awareness. Transformation is what consciousness orchestrates, not compromise.

In our polarized human experience, modern opinions become absolute, with the seemingly unavoidable commandment to align with one or the other. Here's one of my favorites:

"Technology will save us."
or
"Technology will destroy us."

We see this portrayed in films of dystopian despair. In fact, it's rare to see any depiction of a future world where technology isn't grossly destructive, even when "tomorrow" seems outwardly peaceful, like in the Jeff Bridges film, *The Giver*.[3] Yes, that future scenario *was* peaceful but a rebellious element arose, intended to free citizens from the yoke of spiritless conformity. And we, the viewers, agreed! Of course. Who wants peace at the price of individuality?

Over and over again, technology shows up as the villain. But here's something interesting. Apparently, research done by bio-medical engineers at the University of Minnesota, recently published in the scientific journal *TECHNOLOGY*, demonstrates that *"people who practice yoga and meditation long-term can learn to control a computer with their minds faster and better than people with little or no yoga or meditation experience."*[4]

Fascinating… people controlling technology through meditation. That suggests a novel remedy for enslavement by technology! And it gives us immediate opportunities to interact with our machines in a different way. This is not an entirely unfamiliar concept. Many of us have had cars that we loved (especially when we were teenagers!) and sometimes even named. They were like pets and often behaved that way, serving us faithfully long after the physical components should have given out. On the opposite side of that coin are experiences of such alienation from technology that sophisticated equipment refuses to work for us. It's a leap to consider it but there's evidence that attitude does affect supposedly inanimate objects.

From the study itself: *"Brain-computer interface (BCI) systems allow users to interact with their environment by bypassing muscular control to tap directly into the users' thoughts."*[5] This opens up a fascinating possibility:

What if a sustainable future involved detailed cooperation between human and artificial intelligence?

INSIGHT

True wisdom resides beyond
biology and technology.
I am that "more" and I can express love
in each living moment.

ACTION

Focus your attention
on your smart phone or computer.
Sense the connection you have,
biology with technology.

Celebrate the synergistic partnership
between biology and technology.

THE TECHNOLOGY OF NOW

"Beware the barrenness of a busy life."[1]
- Socrates

Who isn't busy in the 21st Century? Contrary to predictions decades old now, technology has not eased our schedules. We're busier than ever and much of that busyness involves the very technology that was predicted to free us. We live bound to our mobile devices, our computers, our screens at work and at home, receiving and transmitting constant updates, staying "connected," while disconnection increases with even our closest friends, with nature, and with our own souls.

Is it really vital to know every trivial detail of our friends lives on Facebook? What's the point of following news stories that run like playoff games… only the last few minutes (few days) really matter. It's one thing to stay informed, a good idea, it's another to surrender to the barrage of useless information that confronts us 24/7 and threatens our serenity at every turn.

There is more background "noise" than ever before in the history of our species. We can't know even a fraction of what's competing for our attention. We hear and see, smell, feel, and touch, but what about the broad range of frequencies beyond the perception of our five senses? What about microwaves, EMF radiation, and odorless toxins? What about the thoughts and feelings of seven billion people? We live in a thrashing sea of environmental influences, many of them toxic. It's easy and socially acceptable to be addictively enrolled in the "pursuit of happiness" (out there), a daily routine that overwhelms our experience of self and marginalizes our awareness of anything but consumer fever. Beware the barrenness of a busy life, indeed! It can render the "still, small voice" of spirit to an inaccessible whisper. And love? Love for things and others can eclipse our love of self, which is the wellspring of authentic love for all.

Here's a novel challenge: rather than unplugging to escape this technology-driven busyness, how might we remain plugged-in but use technology in more constructive ways? For starters, we can exercise our democratic rights and vote, with our remotes! Sometimes it's as simple as changing channels from a high-speed chase to a Japanese garden. There are choices to make and the menu of possibilities has been expanding. Meditators make movies and they write books, they blog and they tweet. Content is a many-splendored thing and we can even narrow our search preferences to participate in conscious networks with those who share our values.

Technology doesn't need to be an enemy. It is a valid aspect of consciousness. Surely it's the pinnacle of pseudo-spiritual delusion to claim that "all is one," yet simultaneously reject technology! Consciousness is not stupid. It doesn't make mistakes. Technology itself is not a mistake, but we must choose how to use it. That begins with acknowledging that it's not an evil to escape from, just as it can never be our savior.

*What if technology is a healthy
evolutionary advance?*

INSIGHT
*Technology is not evil and unplugging
is not the only way to "meditate."
I am becoming what I am destined to become.*

ACTION
*Hold your phone or touch your computer.
Notice if this "object" comes to life in your awareness.*

Celebrate a future of cooperation with technology.

THE PATHLESS PATH

"Transcend the personal mind
and find universal mind.
The personal mind is tied to the ego,
and the ego is forever swinging
from pleasure to pain and back again.
But if you look at awareness
when there is no pleasure or pain,
when the mind is calm while simply existing,
a fascinating journey begins.
You have made the first step on the pathless path."[1]
- Buddha

If technology allows us to show up any way we wish on-line, is that a phenomenon restricted to technology or is it a reflection of something we are already doing unconsciously in real life?

Technology opens up realms of possibilities: "since we can do it… we will." Think about our history and the effect of the internal combustion engine, clear-cutting rain forests, splitting the atom, etc. What about ourselves? How are we using technology to hide from the plight of our world? Are we addicted to gaining pleasure and avoiding pain, with little thought to the broader consequences of our actions, or are we motivated from a deeper level, aligned with the "universal mind?" What guides our choices for who we intend to be, moment by moment?

Just as there are special keys on our keyboards like CONTROL and OPTION and COMMAND that produce instant effects when we strike them, there are personal triggers inside our own "wiring" that get activated by circumstances and choice. The difference is that we choose what we type. Our reactions to "what triggers us" is unconscious and automatic.

Example: someone disrespects or slights you. This can happen in any number of ways, from an oversight at work to an undeserved, unkind word from your spouse, or a newscast with disturbing revelations of corruption in high places. Do you react unconsciously, adding to the abuse in subtle or overt ways? Or do you pause and make a different choice? You might forgive, comfort, even offer kindness instead.

We're not born with this ability but it *is* born in us as potential. To actualize that potential usually takes the help of inspiring mentors who can help us develop our moral compass, to find our "true north," and be guided in our momentary choices to rise above ego reactions and be authentic.

Your choice to be authentic means taking a stand for yourself, to be yourself. This accelerates the process of personal transformation, which must come in the "operating system" itself, deep within our inner wiring. Unless that is changed, we will continue to produce variations-on-the-same-old-theme reactions, rather than be our genuine selves.

What can we do when we are triggered? Remember. Take a breath and remember that we have a choice. Just as we can choose to strike another key on our computer keyboard, we can select another reaction. Making such a choice, over and over again, entrains a new habit in us, until it becomes more natural to be ourselves (no matter what) rather than to collapse into ego dysfunction in defense of the very false self of which we wish to rid ourselves.

What if you could transcend ego reactions and live in universal mind?

INSIGHT
*Avoiding pain and gaining pleasure
are not the only motivations.
I can align with universal mind
and express my true self.*

ACTION
*Today at work, notice when you are triggered.
Choose to express love.*

Celebrate your growing mastery.

PLUG IN

"We are earthlings. The earth is our origin, our nourishment, our support, our guide. Our spirituality itself is Earth–derived. If there is no spirituality in the earth, then there is no spirituality in ourselves."[1]
- Thomas Berry

What is the cure for our modern maladies? They are many, offered to address everything from curing physical diseases to fighting terrorism. There are many proposals but when it comes to personal stress management, we're often told to unplug. Meditate, breathe, be mindful, and practice yoga. Turn off your computer, take a break from texting, and retreat from busyness into silence. Such is the modern call towards finding balanced wellbeing in the high-tech 21st Century.

"Getting away from it all" worked for centuries, back when life was simple and the earth was sparsely populated, when civilization and technology were unimagined dreams. A mystic could meditate for hours in his cave, bathing in the electromagnetic waves of the earth—known today as the Schumann Resonances— being sustained in balance within a cavity that reaches from the surface of the earth up 55 kilometers to the inner edge of the ionosphere.

Fast forward to the 21st century and it's a different landscape in every way: seven billion people, endless expanses of concrete and steel, and electromagnetic pollution permeating the atmosphere, with nary a cave in sight.

Those who advise us to unplug are uninformed as to why traditional meditative techniques worked. Mystics of old didn't find 20 minutes before a board meeting. They didn't practice mindfulness during the drive to pick up their kids from preschool. They weren't breathing consciously on the subway or while stuck in traffic. They had time and space, and their lives weren't fragmented between a thousand diverse activities. Most important, they were able to experience states of expanded awareness because they lived in an unpolluted environment.

Unplugging from technology is now impossible. And meditating "ain't what it used to be." Something different is called for, not just to unplug from busyness but to plug in to life, to the natural world. Remember that world, the environment we've treated as an inert, unintelligent backdrop for our magnificent creating?

We've learned to filter out nature. For many people, nature is incidental. Unless you live in a forest, it takes deliberate effort to connect with the natural world. Some people bicycle to work, many jog in the park. But what's the purpose? Is it to save on gas, get exercise and fresh air, or is there more? Is this the opportunity to reconnect, to meditate in unique ways by interacting with the world we arose from and still owe our existence to?

Instead of just unplugging, we can plug in to this world we've neglected and come to feel again the sustaining power of this neighborhood of thriving life that lives around and within us. From micro-organisms to distant stars, it's all "nature." Let's meditate on that!

What if meditation became your "we" activity?

INSIGHT
*Unplugging from technology is not enough.
I can experience community by
plugging in to the natural world.*

ACTION
*Take a walk today and pause to touch a tree,
close your eyes and shift your point of view
to within, connected, not separate.*

Celebrate your oneness with life in all its forms.

ANYTHING IS POSSIBLE

"The development of quantum mechanics early in the twentieth century obliged physicists to change radically the concepts they used to describe the world."[1]
- Alain Aspect

The primary revelation: anything is possible!

One of the fascinating revelations of quantum science is the "observer effect." Simply put, we've learned that the way we observe changes the nature of what we perceive. Some see the glass half-full, some see it half-empty. And so it is.

There is an old story that demonstrates this well: *"Two shoe salesmen were sent to Africa to see if there was a market for their product. The first salesman reported back, 'This is a terrible business opportunity, no-one wears shoes.' The second salesman reported back, 'This is a fantastic business opportunity, no-one wears shoes.'"[2]*

One saw opportunity, the other saw none. The situation was identical; the way of seeing was different. So, what do we see? More specifically, what do we choose to see? And, do we take an active role in changing our perception?

Meditation, the traditional "sit," helps a person calm their thinking, to alter their perception, to bring order to their inner world. If peace increases, how long can this meditative state be maintained after they open their eyes? Here is a second discipline: ongoing mindfulness. This produces a consistent state of altered perception.

When someone develops the ability to sustain their meditative state, it transforms the nature and the potency of their attention and generates a transformative impact on their experienced reality.

Someone like the Dalai Lama brings a focus of cheerfulness and appreciation into every situation. Anyone who has been in his presence reports the impact. Just one look, a smile from a distance, or a kind touch on the shoulder, changed their lives forever. It might even be subtler than that. His energy field is the first level of impact.

The broadcast frequency of his attention/intention doesn't happen by accident and neither does yours. But there's more involved here than personality and genius. Any person can develop the ability to sustain focus this way. Miraculous events will begin to unfold because of the quality of their attention/intention. Literally, anything can happen, as many people can attest to.

I recall a friend describing how he and his wife were moving to another country and had secured a new home for their beloved cats. At the last moment, the plan fell through. On the eve of their departure, they faced the tragedy of abandoning their feline children to a shelter. Suddenly the phone rang. A stranger was calling about an entirely different matter. My friend was moved to mention their heartache. This prompted an excited response. "I've been looking for two cats. I'll take them!" A prayer was answered in the most unlikely fashion.

Discoveries in the mysterious quantum world explain this kind of phenomenon. That prayer broadcast out and attracted in exactly what was needed. Different results in life depend on the degree to which any of us choose to take personal responsibility for the quality of our expression. The Dalai Lama is cheerful and direct and that produces a consistent impact. He models how much one person can do, from the inside out. What's possible for you and me if we learn to focus our attention and perceive in new ways?

What if you embraced the idea that
anything is possible in life?

INSIGHT

There are two kinds of meditation:
the "sit" and mindfulness.
I am a creative presence.

ACTION

Focus your attention during a "sit" meditation.
Afterwards, focus your intention
through mindfulness.
Sustain your meditative state.

Celebrate your choice to consciously
develop a meaningful life.

EXPECT THE UNEXPECTED

"The ever-accelerating progress of technology ...
gives the appearance
of approaching some essential singularity
in the history of the race
beyond which human affairs, as we know them,
could not continue."[1]
- John von Neumann

Singularity is defined in many ways, but generally refers to a future phenomenon, a technological *"moment"* where laws that have governed *"reality"* break down. In other words: the ultimate uncertainty.

Author and futurist Ray Kurzweil predicts: *"... a future period during which the pace of technological change will be so rapid, its impact so deep, that human life will be irreversibly transformed. Although neither utopian nor dystopian, this epoch will transform the concepts that we rely on to give meaning to our lives, from our business models to the cycle of human life, including death itself."[2]*

I would submit that this epoch is already upon us. Familiar concepts we once relied on to give meaning to the world are fast becoming obsolete. For instance, "distance" has been redefined by modern communication and travel. Weather changes are demanding adaptation. Increasingly, our entire human status quo is being challenged: job security is basically gone (who has just one career anymore?); economic "progress" is stalling (for the first time in history American children are less well off than their parents); and previously vanquished diseases like measles, malaria and tuberculosis are making a comeback (sparking controversy over the long term effectiveness of vaccines). What in the world is the world coming to?

Evidence suggests we should expect the unexpected! When it comes, we struggle to "right the ship" and to re-establish a previously known equilibrium. But this traditional strategy may—at some point in the near future—fail. Perhaps it already is, spelling the end of the status quo, no more "business as usual."

Buckminster Fuller said, *"Man is going to be displaced altogether as a specialist by the computer. Man himself is being forced to reestablish, employ, and enjoy his innate 'comprehensivity.' Coping with the totality of Spaceship Earth and universe is ahead for all of us."*[3]

What might this entail? We don't know. We can't know. But what might we imagine? For one thing, even reading Fuller's description can expand our thinking. Spaceship Earth... we are riding through the cosmos in a spaceship! What a realization. And did you know that the earth moves around the sun at the speed of 67,000 miles per hour? That's 18.5 miles per second! Yet, it feels like we aren't moving at all.

Simultaneously, we are moving through space. And space itself is moving. Very quickly the whole reality becomes mind boggling. And that's a good thing. It might help prepare us for what lies ahead in our future... something unexpected! They say that the wise man trusts Allah *and* ties up his camel. This sounds like a balanced approach to whatever lies ahead. Instead of fearing the unexpected, what if we anticipated surprises and prepared for them? How might that sharpen our ability to adapt?

What if you expected the unexpected?

INSIGHT
Transformation for humanity is happening already and it is inevitable.
I am a conscious participant in the greatest adventure in human history.

ACTION
Expect the unexpected today.
Choose new behaviors.

Celebrate your courage and creativity.

BEYOND THE CAVE

"Attention span is the amount of concentrated time on
a task without becoming distracted. Most educators and
psychologists agree that the ability to focus attention
on a task is crucial for the achievement of one's goals.
It's no surprise attention spans have been
decreasing over the past decade
with the increase in external stimulation."[1]
- Michael Brenner

Thousands of years ago, spiritual masters meditated in caves. The earth was sparsely populated and there was virtually no electronic technology sabotaging their experience of deep and abiding peace. Mystics needed little to survive.

The basics remain in place: meditation, breathing, mindfulness… the same powerful techniques used for centuries to create a soulful life are valid today, even though we endure more distractions and interferences than at any other time in human history. It's more accurate to call it pollution. And this requires a new strategy.

Here in the 21st century, the question is either, "How can I escape the noise and busyness OR how can I adapt to the modern reality and find peace in different ways?"

The ancients lived in an environment where their brains weren't being constantly bombarded by data and stimulation and radiation. Information was presented in long, slow chunks (just watch an old movie… the pace is glacial!). Fast forward to today (at least to 2013 when these statistics were assembled) when the National Center for Biotechnology Information at the U.S. National Library of Medicine informs us that, since the year 2000, our average attention span has dropped from 12 seconds to 8 seconds, a 33% decrease.[2]   Goldfish, by the way, have an attention span of 9 seconds, one better than us!

No wonder sitting meditation is so difficult! With an attention span of 8 seconds, it's dizzying to speculate how many random thoughts might float through in a 20-minute session. Finding refuge on the inside isn't as easy as it used to be.

Here's an alternative, beyond "the cave." What if our decreasing attention span was also a sign of evolutionary growth? After all, what are we supposed to be paying attention to? Isn't it the content of the moment, and isn't that increasingly diverse? What if your attention was *meant* to shift, not in fragmented dysfunction but in a harmonious dance? What if you learned to focus attention in a radically different way?

Could it be that civilization is not the enemy of "enlightenment?" What if consciousness did not make a mistake by inventing the modern world? What if everything carries the potential to contribute to the expansion of human awareness?

Let's imagine this is so. Is there a downside to that attitude? If so, it's difficult to find. "Seek and ye shall find," has long been the instruction. What we seek tends to determine what we find. If we put off enlightenment into the realm of future attainment, we will always labor on the path. But if we embrace the illumination of the moment and take personal responsibility to *be* the light, not to *find* the light, then... this is it!

What if every moment were 'it?'

INSIGHT
*The modern world challenges us with distractions
that ancient sages never had.
I am able to focus my attention now.*

ACTION
*Take a stroll through your neighborhood, walk slowly.
Returning home, look in a mirror.
What do you see in yourself that you never saw before?*

*Celebrate your commitment
to seeing through new eyes.*

YOUR FIRST HOME

*"Except the Lord build the house,
they labor in vain that build it."[1]*
- Psalm 127

Homelessness is reaching epidemic proportions in our modern world. According to a report from the United Nations Commission on Human Rights, there were 100 million homeless people world-wide in 2005. More recent estimates now range upwards of 200 million. In America, 13% of homeless people have jobs but still can't afford housing and, of the estimated 2.5 million homeless people in the U.S., 1.37 million are children under 18.[2]

These are shocking statistics. America is supposed to be leading the way, but not this way! How could this happen in the land of the brave and free? What did we miss for the last century? Actually, it's a spiritual problem. If we are not living in harmony with life in the universe, if we are not building our individual house of being according to the organic, synergistic, ever-fluctuating blueprint alive everywhere in the universe, no wonder homelessness increases. We are *not* at home, we are alienated. The statistics are a reflection of this inner state.

All the wonders of our modern world ... yet millions of our own children have no homes. Literally. Surely that stirs us to compassion and determination to contribute to something better in the world.

Do you ever feel homeless, even though you have a home? Many people do, even the wealthy. Ironically, some without houses—living on the street or wandering the world—report a sense of belonging, beyond the confines of any structure. They've rediscovered their first home, the energetic field they live in 24/7.

Home resides inside us. We can feel it on the street. We can suffer the absence of it in a mansion. The sense of belonging starts within. It's energy, really. It's emotion. All of us live in a field of invisible energy and it's as unique as our signature.

Recall how you can recognize an old friend you haven't seen in many years. Their appearance may have changed drastically but something about them has remained the same... the way they "feel." We could pick them out in the dark.

Anyone can change their personal energy field. Meditation is a beginning but where does it go from there? How long can we sustain our meditative state during everyday living? This requires "course correction" but that's impossible if we haven't chosen a destination. How would you know which way to turn?

The "destination" is not a geographical location; it's a state of being. And it is always experienced here and now, through being increasingly present right where we are. Developing this ability has a powerful effect on us. In fact, it's essential for a productive, happy life. Look at someone like the Dalai Lama. He's no longer a young man and yet he sustains a schedule that would intimidate most of us half his age. Throughout, he remains cheerful and inspiring and is clearly living with passion. His energy field is legendary, affecting a transformative influence for many he meets. He is thoroughly at home within his own skin. How about us?

What if you felt at home inside your own skin?

INSIGHT
Homelessness is increasing everywhere in the world.
I build my energetic home
by sustaining my connection with source energy.

ACTION
Meditate on feeling at home inside your own skin.

Celebrate your first and eternal home.

Chapter Twelve, March 8   WINTER

INSPIRATION IS THE OXYGEN OF OUR SURVIVAL

"At this very moment, the Earth is above you, below you,
all around you, and even inside you.
The Earth is everywhere.
You may be used to thinking of the Earth as only the ground
beneath your feet. But the water, the sea, the sky,
and everything around us comes from the Earth.
Everything outside us and everything inside us
comes from the Earth. ... We are the Earth and
we are always carrying her within us."[1]
- Thich Nhat Hanh

Inspiration is oxygen for our survival; our minds and hearts and souls need it as much as our bodies need air. Some animals can survive for weeks, even months, without eating physical food. Can our minds and hearts and souls survive without inspiration? Survival, short-term, yes. Thriving long-term, no.

Where does inspiration come from? Use your imagination to answer that! Anywhere and everywhere, obviously. But the neglected source that deserves attention is nature. As the above quote describes, we *are* the earth, we *are* nature. Yet, how disconnected we have become.

Who has time for nature? Busy lives demand loyalty to work, families, etc. We may take holidays and get out for a walk when we can. But being inspired by nature shouldn't be a hobby. It can happen regardless of where we are and it needn't be scheduled. Nature, we can come to experience, is not "out there" and only accessible on special occasions. It surrounds us and it lives inside us.

Nature *is* what we are. To deeply experience this requires a change of perspective. Who are you? If you believe you are wholly contained within your skin, inside this bag of bones and organs, and that everything else – nature for instance – is separate "out there," then it's impossible to experience the oneness Thich Nhat Hanh described.

His words are deeply inspiring. They point to a unique path of enlightenment which is not crowded! You won't encounter traffic jams in nature; more often there's no one there. Seemingly. Actually, it's *all* alive.

It's all alive and we're part of it. We aren't separate from those billions of life forms in nature—around us and within us—and we aren't separate from each other. Did you know that within our bodies bacteria cells outnumber human cells ten to one? Imagine that. There are billions of microscopic life forms living within our bodies, immediately surrounding us, and proliferating everywhere in the cosmos. We're breathing it all in and out in every moment. We are indeed the stuff of stars, the dust of centuries past, the lingering presence of each other through countless incarnations.

Inspiration is the oxygen of our survival. We can transform our lives by using this simple but powerful realization to change our point of view—so that we are "inside and one with," not lonely and "separate from."

What if you experienced yourself being inside nature?

INSIGHT
Humans live in the earth, not on the earth.
I am always in relationship
with trillions of other life forms.

ACTION
Look in the mirror and ask "Who am I?"
Then walk in nature, silently saying, "I am this."

Celebrate your oneness with nature.

PROGRESS

"What good is technological progress
without moral progress?
How about we pause, put down our devices,
look up and listen to our hearts and our consciences?
Not so much 'connectivity' as just connecting
with each other. And if that moral progress could keep pace
with technological progress
then that would be, well, real progress."[1]
- Queen Rania al Abdullah of Jordan

How about forging such a deep connection with the source that unites us all that we become easily able to remain connected whether we are "on-line" or not? In fact, why not reframe that concept to understand that we are *always* on-line, that we are always connected? This may seem exotic; no, it's realistic.

Let's make this shift right now. You are reading, either from a hard copy or on a screen. We are having a certain kind of conversation. I am speaking to you as I write, you are responding back to me as I read, via the range of reactions you have. There is a flow between us and, obviously, it transcends time and space because I wrote this long before the moment you read it and we are not in the same room. But, somehow, we are conversing.

When did you read the last sentence? At that time, it was "now." When will you read the next sentence? In the future? Perhaps, but that moment will also be "now," by the time you get there. Speaking of progress, here we discover a possible breakthrough of immense proportion: liberating ourselves from the tyranny of linear time to experience the eternity of now.

Human time is an invention, after all. It's useful, just as money is useful, but these are tools for effective living, not rules to enslave us. You are reading now. Soon you will be doing something else. If you find connection and immediacy in these moments of reading, will you be able to sustain this sensation during other activities? Distractions abound... but is that what they are? Yes, if we focus in a linear way: "I am doing this and only this." Softening your perception ... spreading out your focus to include everything that is happening (fundamentally different from "multi-tasking") ... sustaining this experience of being on-line in a deeper way. I'm not the first one to call this the "Innernet."

Find kinship with this reality and learn how to appreciate and include everything in every moment as a valid part of our experience (rather than distractions from what we want to get done). Participating in the dance of all... now, *that* would be real progress!

Some refer to this as living in "deep time." Deep time is timeless. Deep time is what we experience in the winter season of our lives, when it's right to contemplate and reflect. But seasons change and now, as we follow the earth in its movement around the sun, we prepare for what comes next, for spring, and the appearance of new life that reminds us that we are ever-connected within this dancing phenomenon we call life.

***What if you measured progress
in terms of increasing connection?***

INSIGHT
*Technology and biology are companions.
I am evolving, always "on-line" in life.*

ACTION
*Study a houseplant closely.
Soften your perception and experience your connection.*

Celebrate your multi-dimensional progress.

WINTER FLOWS INTO SPRING

Winter is passing and spring is coming.

Spring … the sprouting of seeds, growth in the world and evolution in yourself … the inevitable outcome of accessing inner truth and bringing it into a fuller expression of celebration and transformation within yourself. Spring bursts forth from winter's gestation, flooding all dimensions of your being.

In springtime, you awaken more fully to the fact that you have been mired in illusion, that you have glimpsed the truth, and your life now is about building truth. This is the basis of all wisdom traditions and that wisdom is alive in you now.

Everything in your life will now support this evolution. Your first and foremost practice is meditation but there are many forms. All of them increase balance and expand awareness so you can now stay awake, growing the dominance of love over fear and truth over illusion.

Spring brings a blossoming of love for yourself. This is how you are increasingly able to experience love for others. They, like you, have been seduced and suffocated in the embrace of an illusory "self," complete with wounds from childhood. Can you love yourself as you are? Can you accept others as they are, knowing the same life that empowers you all?

You have nothing without this life force. Celebrate the coming spring of your expanding awareness, simply being alive and loving the experience of life you have. Rise from your slumbers in illusion, your own personal hibernation.

It's time to rise and shine!

PART TWO

WELCOME TO SPRING

WELCOME TO SPRING

"Living together is an art."[1]
- Thich Nhat Hanh

Spring is the season of emergence, the sprouting of the seed, the renewal of life.

A similar cycle is operative in all of us. Spring comes as we access the truth and bring it into a fuller expression within ourselves. Emerging from the gestation season of winter comes expanding awareness, bursting forth, flooding all dimensions of our being.

Hibernating animals awaken in spring. Likewise, humanity has been asleep, mired in illusion, and it is now awakening. We glimpsed this truth in our winter dream; now millions of us stir, awaken, and begin to build our truthful experience. Awakening is the metaphor in all wisdom traditions, then developing the dominance of truth over illusion, changing the primary experience from fear to love.

Meditation, in all its forms, is our best ally in this transition. First things first, and that means balance and expanding awareness within the midst of our busy lives. Life accelerates in spring—all the more reason to be deliberate about attending to our inner experience, to continue building the dominance of love over fear, of truth over illusion.

The first priority in our awakening is to learn to love ourselves. This is what enables us to love others. We must love ourselves first, before we can experience the same love with anyone or anything else.

That's "easier said than done" for most of us, who've survived abused childhoods and disempowering programming, who battle inner demons and try to ignore those inner voices that tell us how unlovable we really are. Nevertheless, we are dismantling an illusory identity, so we can relinquish trying to make what is counterfeit into who we already are.

This lovability challenge afflicts us all. Everyone is experiencing the same illusory self-negation that decimates self-worth, self-acceptance, and self-love. Meditation is not an escape—it's a portal, an opening into a deeper exploration of what is fundamentally true about the self. As you awaken and stretch your spring self, take the first step: love yourself. Love yourself, not because you are suddenly free of all you feared that made you feel unworthy but because you embrace the truth of yourself beyond that illusory identity ... and because you expand your awareness of what love really is.

Can you love the life that empowers you? Can you embrace the experience of life that gives you everything? Can you get in touch with being alive and loving the experience of life that makes all this possible?

Strip away the distractions and go to the source. *This* is the real point of meditation. *This* is what it means to love yourself. You learn that love is your very nature and open to the loving energy that already empowers you, the love that you already are. Once you experience that, illusions of self-worth begin to crumble. And, not surprisingly, your experience of love with others expands. You begin to live together in love. How could it be otherwise?

Most relationships are based in the illusion of separation. They are subject / object relationships. From an egocentric perspective, all of these are exploitive. When you look at relationships from a truthful perspective and shift to subject / subject relationships, they become respectful. The difference between illusion and truth is profound.

This change promotes an increased amplitude of personal power, much more than you are accustomed to, and it impacts all aspects of your life, every relationship. The expanding influence of your love expression ripples through every level of your multidimensional being. When it encounters that which is incongruent (a limited experience of love and identity), it will appear "in your face" so you can look at it, see it for what it is, and discard it. Fear not, spring has sprung!

Illumination, spiritual evolution, and personal transformation are as inevitable as this turning of the seasons.

Chapter Fourteen, March 22   SPRING

THE POWER OF CHOICE

"You should sit in meditation for twenty minutes
every day — unless you're too busy.
Then you should sit for an hour."[1]
- Zen proverb

Has meditating become a luxury most people can't afford? Keeping pace with the world of today can leave little time for sitting. Or, as the proverb instructed, is being busy all the more reason to get off the merry-go-round more regularly and for longer periods?

While it may have become habitual to feel overwhelmed by the busyness of 21st century life, we *do* have a choice about where we direct our attention and how we spend our time. And time (as we know it) is largely perception. Einstein explained his theory of relativity in layman's terms this way: "Put your hand on a hot stove for a minute, and it seems like an hour. Sit with a pretty girl for an hour, and it seems like a minute. That's relativity."[2]

We all make time for pleasure, for activities we desire. If meditation is a duty, you won't do it for long. If meditation is something you believe you should want to do and try, you will fail. That's not meditation. Meditation is not an activity you decide to do. Real meditation is the fulfillment of an internal process, satisfying a hunger for connection with source that compels a person to interrupt their involvement with the external world and go within. Why? To be "fed," in response to what I've described in my last two books as "The Awakening Impulse."

Is it in you? Here's how you know: you're reading these words! Words that encourage more awakening hold no appeal to those who have not already been moved by this "Impulse." It may have moved you ... to read this book!

This awakening impulse can be deliberately intensified through choice. An old t-shirt comes to mind, with its inscription: "Everyone must believe in something; I believe I'll have another beer." What do you believe in? Do you choose activities that deepen your experience of life, like meditation, or is "another beer" more satisfying? There's a time and place for everything but the sum total of our choices throughout life determines the journey we take and the nature of our final destination.

Short-term fulfillment is exactly that. What lasts is honoring the evolutionary urge within us which, when heeded, propels us steadily into life's depth. And that water is sweeter! Sweet satisfaction… to know that one is drinking as deeply as possible from the water of life.

Busyness tends to keep us on the surface, going wide. Mindfulness orients us into depth, and the sort of intimacy that nourishes our very souls. Isn't it ironic that something as simple as closing our eyes and being present could be so fulfilling? But every authentic meditator knows this pleasure. What began somewhere in personal history as a choice becomes an imperative and the meditative state persists longer and longer between sessions until finally that last remaining sliver between "sits" vanishes in the consistency of sustained bliss.

What if you chose to meditate every day,
with no exceptions?

INSIGHT
Extreme busyness sends a message:
increase meditation time.
I choose awakening.

ACTION
Finish reading this entry and meditate.

Celebrate your ability to choose awakening.

Chapter Fifteen, March 29   SPRING

THE MEDITATION ADVANTAGE

"When we raise ourselves through meditation
to what unites us with the spirit,
we quicken something within us that is
eternal and unlimited by birth and death.
Once we have experienced this eternal part in us,
we can no longer doubt its existence.
Meditation is thus the way to knowing and beholding
the eternal, indestructible, essential center of our being."[1]
- Rudolf Steiner

The gulf between science and spirit continues to close, as a *Psychology Today* article confirms. *"In a very real way, you literally are changing your brain for the better when you meditate... In the end, this means that you are able to see yourself and everyone around you from a clearer perspective, while simultaneously being more present, compassionate and empathetic with people no matter the situation. With time and practice, people do truly become calmer, have a greater capacity for empathy and find they tend to respond in a more balanced way to things, people or events in their lives."[2]*

Brainwaves are measured in frequency (the speed of electrical pulses) and in amplitude (strength). A meditation practice increases amplitude, expanding Alpha and Theta frequencies. Strengthened Alpha waves indicate a sustained meditative state, lasting throughout waking hours (not just during "sits"). This produces an expanded sense of personal presence, the timeless sensation of being.

The *Psychology Today* article emphasizes that to sustain what you gain during meditation you have to keep doing it. Why? Because of the brain's neuroplasticity, it can easily and quickly revert back to its old habits. Ongoing meditation ensures that those new neural pathways you are developing remain in place and stay strong.

In his book, *Outliers*,[3] Malcolm Gladwell wrote that it takes 10,000 hours of practice to become "world class" at something. Let's measure that. If you were to meditate one hour per day, that's 30 years! Sounds daunting. But the math changes very quickly if one hour turns into four or ten. The secret is consistency. Some habit experts recommend five to six weeks of daily practice to create a new habit. Meditation is one habit, committing to extend the meditative state is another. Those who've chosen this path know it happens in stages, with a new commitment required at each new level of experience. Down we drop, deeper and deeper into the simple bliss of the moment.

In a world where most things are beyond our personal control, it's empowering to know that the simple act of meditation can develop a significant advantage in living. Challenges that defeat many people can be taken in stride by the veteran meditator, who has developed the ability to maintain equilibrium amidst the most severe crises and continues to offer a peace-enhancing influence into their environment.

What does a sustained meditative state look like? One simple description is "patience." Often a solution is found simply by waiting. But it's an active kind of waiting… pausing to drop deeper into the moment and access a wisdom that is present but only available to those with the bandwidth to perceive it. One becomes a detective of life, learning how to sleuth out solutions from the wisdom of life itself.

***What if you used meditation as a strategy
for crisis management?***

INSIGHT
*Meditation changes the brain.
I choose to enhance my cognitive abilities
and intuitive wisdom through regular meditation.*

ACTION
*Meditate today
twice as long as you usually do.*

Celebrate your evolving brain.

Chapter Sixteen, April 5   SPRING

You're Smarter Than You Think

*"I know that I am intelligent,
because I know that I know nothing."[1]*
- Socrates

History tells us that Socrates won his debates by challenging rivals to prove what they believed they knew. They couldn't. In this way, he proved that knowing is not just about acquiring, storing, and defending knowledge, it is about accessing understanding that emerges fresh and relevant in the moment.

An online dictionary defines The Socratic Method as *"a teaching technique in which a teacher does not give information directly but instead asks a series of questions, with the result that the student comes either to the desired knowledge by answering the questions or to a deeper awareness of the limits of knowledge."[2]*

To claim true knowledge you must first confess to not knowing. You do this by asking questions. For instance, you might ask yourself, "How can I accelerate the expansion of my awareness?"

Such a question opens a space for new knowing to arise. You can ask any question you like. And you can do it any time. For instance, you're stuck in traffic. You could interview yourself with simple questions like: "Who supports my personal growth and who doesn't?" That could lead to adjustments in your social circle. You can engage in this kind of self-inquiry when you're drifting off to sleep or first thing in the morning, before you arise and plug in to another busy day. Any question that probes your life experience will work.

There is no end to this kind of self-inquiry. Done consistently, it becomes a life affirming habit. There's something inherently appealing about any person who lives in questions. They carry an openness, they live in spaciousness, and they inspire exploration in those they meet.

Starting from "not knowing," your awareness expands into knowing. For instance, that gut sense about who amongst family and friends supports the truly important aspects of your life (and who doesn't) might deliver some surprises! And, some change.

If a new understanding develops, where did it come from? It existed, somewhere, before you asked the questions, but asking was required for you to make your knowing conscious. That's expansion. As the Bible says, *"Ask, and it shall be given you."*[3] In other words, you are smarter than you think. Thinking—from an existing database of knowing—isn't what makes you smart. You are smarter than that, *if* you learn how to access the limitless database available to those with humble minds. As French philosopher Blaise Pascal famously remarked, *"Small minds are concerned with the extraordinary, great minds with the ordinary."*[4]

Certainly, the extraordinary is dazzling. Some meditators become preoccupied with extraordinary experiences while meditating. But veterans come to cherish the ordinary moments, the absolutely calm surface of the lake of their minds.

Calm and contentment are not achieved through busyness that finally gets everything under control! Techniques may be offered that promise that kind of mastery but the real secret is simple: be… here… now. Those words sound familiar! Indeed, they have been uttered in one way or another for many centuries. And, we still have much to learn about what they really mean.

What if you traded knowing for learning?

INSIGHT
Wisdom is not measured in knowing,
it's measured in learning.
I am wise when I surrender what I have known
in favor of what I am discovering.

ACTION
Practice asking yourself questions.

Celebrate your humility.

Chapter Seventeen, April 12   SPRING

NATURE IS NEVER IN DEBT

"The road to hell is paved with good intentions,
heaven is full of good works."[1]
- Anonymous

The saying *"The road to hell is paved with good intentions"* is thought to have originated with Saint Bernard of Clairvaux around 1150 A.D. but is predated by other researchers back to Virgil's "Aeneid." In other words, this understanding has been around for a long time... but we are still ignoring it!

The worst of good intentions are those that ignore nature. While we could make a long list of ways that we've done that over the centuries (starting with our peculiar ignorance of the sun as an energy source), here's a fascinating truth to ponder: there is no debt in nature.

This is starkly unlike human systems where profit is the goal and debt is the result. Profit is measured in accumulation—that's the human way—and that creates debt. In nature, the norm is distribution. In our human economy, more is better; in nature, balance is best. There is no hoarding and there is no debt in nature—these are extremes that we invented. Nature is balanced and generous. Every plant produces an abundance of seeds and shares them without generating obligation. Likewise, the sun shines on all, demanding nothing in return.

It's actually a much simpler system. Imagine not keeping track of transactions? The growing phenomenon of time-exchange systems is proving that people are naturally generous with each other. These alternate currency organizations track giving and receiving in hours, not dollars. But history shows that many of them dissolve into unrecorded exchanges between friends and neighbors who have grown to trust universal math... that everything evens out in the end, even when it doesn't!

One of the secrets of such systems is that while they are usually local—between people who know each other—they are also infinite in the sense that giving is experienced as wealth-generating somewhere with someone. The value doesn't need to be computed and accounted for in obvious ways. True giving, with no strings attached, creates a field where true receiving (wholly voluntary on the part of the giver) is attracted. What a different economy this suggests!

And, of course, that's how it happens in nature all the time! There are no accountants in the forest. So, how do we connect with this world we've ignored and develop a new relationship? We can do this with nature walks, obviously. But let's also consider a specific kind of meditation. For centuries, meditation has served as the primary tool to regain connection with source. It can also be a technique for deepening personal connection with the inherent magic of natural systems—especially if we do our "sit" outside (weather permitting). The environment begins to change in us, rendering us able to think and act in harmony with nature, the polar opposite of having good intentions generated from our heads. In the end, it's actions that count. Actions arise from intentions. What kind of intentions inspire our actions—good intentions that pave the road to hell or natural thinking that brings balance?

What if you learned to think in concert with nature?

INSIGHT
Thinking separate from nature produces hell.
I can align my thinking with nature and produce heaven.

ACTION
Meditate in nature. Invite the sights, sounds and smells,
the feel of the natural world
to revive the primal wisdom in your very cells.

Celebrate your intelligence as part of the natural world.

LOVE IS A CHOICE

"We're going to have to be serious to add enough
of the feminine into the patriarchy
so that what emerges is neither a patriarchy
nor a matriarchy, but a human–archy.
And not even that. What we need is a being–archy,
where all beings are granted
mutual respect and where decisions are made
with the whole circle of life in mind."[1]
- Elizabeth Lesser

The crisis of our times is calling for an individual and species-wide shift into a more love-based, compassionate expression of consciousness. This involves becoming more sensitive to every aspect and detail of our lives, such as nature around us, the food we eat, our exercise, what we read, what we watch, our relationships, our occupation and how we work.

When any person chooses to make this shift a priority, they automatically become more selective. They become a "conscious" individual, and that's how society becomes more discriminating, one person at a time. Of course, "one person" only becomes a real force for change when that one person is "me." Here in the 21st century we are witnessing a virtual tsunami of personal accountability, as more and more individuals do step up and commit themselves to "me-first" activism.

To work, this must lead to balance. What any individual does to improve their own lives or communities or the world at large is done in alignment with—not independent of—all beings in the living environment. Personal actions reveal a balance of masculine and feminine, focus and flow, being and doing.

This is what love is, really—the balanced and lively interaction of yin and yang everywhere in human experience and throughout the cosmos. That we have ignored love and steamrollered through the environment with macho achievement attitudes is obvious and shameful. Look at what we have done to the world.

Love (experiencing love) is a choice. Living in the balance of masculine and feminine—and in respectful relationship with all beings—is a choice. It's one that increasing numbers of individuals are making, swept along by what I call the Awakening Impulse. This is the evolutionary tide that is moving humanity. Our species is transforming. Humanity 1.0 is becoming as obsolete as the dinosaurs that once ruled the world. They went extinct. Suddenly. Will that be our fate? Will Humanity 1.0 be the only version, or are we upgrading to Humanity 2.0? If so, what might that look like?

The more consciously awake we become, the more willing we are to share with each other. Note the explosion of networking through social media. That's a sign. But something deeper than talking about what we had for lunch and posting pictures of our pets is called for. The Awakening Impulse is stirring us to go deeper and, when we honor it, the choice to love propels us into new relationships with all who yearn in the same ways we do.

What if you became "conscious"
and chose true love in your relationships?

INSIGHT
We are part of the circle of life, which includes all beings.
I am one, in love, with all beings everywhere.

ACTION
Introduce more depth into your interactions on social media.
Be a thought leader, inviting and facilitating
conversations that matter.

Celebrate your courage.

THE GREAT RACE

*"Just because something doesn't do what you planned
it to do doesn't mean it's useless."[1]*
- Thomas Edison

AI stands for artificial intelligence (computers and robots). IA stands for intelligence augmentation (e.g., learning Spanish overnight). A recent essay warned: *"A big question is which field will advance faster? And how big is the lag time between them? I would admit that right now it appears as if AI is leaping ahead of IA and there is reason to be concerned. But this is not necessarily written in stone."[2]*

There are plenty of science fiction movies depicting dystopian futures where AI has enslaved humanity (*Terminator*, etc.). But this is not written in stone. Our future may turn out to be something fundamentally different from what it is widely feared to be. It's entertaining, and we seem to have an endless appetite for feasts of future carnage, but is there an alternative, in reality?

We don't see much evidence of that possibility, certainly not in films. There are hundreds of depictions of future alienation and conformists prisons but very few that might give us hope. In fact, *2001, A Space Odyssey* is about the only one I could think of!

What film makers and researchers fail to factor into their projections is consciousness itself. In fact, the idea that consciousness has an influence is roundly ignored. That's interesting, given that all essential life functions are orchestrated by consciousness, without help from our intellects and egos. Without our interference, consciousness does a great job and I doubt we'd be arrogant enough to believe we could do better with our technology. Anyone care to volunteer to beat their own heart for a day or even a minute? How about regenerating liver cells, growing hair and fingernails, and keeping the planet in orbit?

What might consciousness have in mind for the future? Consciousness created both biology and technology. What looks like a great race, with only one winner/survivor, becomes a fundamentally different scenario when you consider the two in partnership rather than competition. AI is not a threat and IA is not a defense. Our future can be a merger of the two: Humanity 2.0.

What Humanity might be like is not a total mystery. To survive, all species adapt to changing conditions. What if that's what's happening now, not a challenge to survive but a challenge to adapt? Survival comes, or not, depending on adaptation. If we consider our official leadership, there is reason for discouragement! How long does it take for change to take hold? I've read that it takes about 20 years for an acknowledged breakthrough in the medical field to be officially adopted as a best practice. And let's not talk politics!

It's up to us, ordinary people who don't have as much of a commitment to the status-quo or business-as-usual. This is the source of true leadership arising in the 21st century. It's up to us to imagine a bright future and shine our way there!

What if the future isn't dark?

INSIGHT
Biology and technology are not competing for survival.
I am merging biology and technology
to become a new human.

ACTION
Machines are alive. Every time you touch one,
acknowledge your kin.

Celebrate your partnership as a new human being.

FORWARD

*"Technological progress has merely provided us
with more efficient means for going backwards."[1]*
- Aldous Huxley

While scientists and movie makers simultaneously rave and tremble about the impact technology is having on our planet and the failing chances for human survival, consciousness has its own game plan.

Whether humans will get smart enough fast enough (through IA, which stands for intelligence augmentation) to withstand the challenge of AI (artificial intelligence) is a debate that misses that central point. Consciousness is orchestrating its own game plan.

Futurist Ray Kurzweil proposed that, *"When you talk to a human in 2035, you'll be talking to someone that's a combination of biological and non-biological intelligence."[2]* Kurzweil has faith in our ability to co-inhabit the planet peaceably. Others in the know aren't so confident. For them, it is a great race... and AI is winning. In fact, experts warn that beyond a certain point AI can't be controlled. That's not a happy moment for humans, they warn. Predictions point to enslavement by unfeeling machines. *"Resistance is futile!"[3]* was the warning from The Borg in *Star Trek*, as this machine consciousness marched across the galaxies, absorbing organic life forms into its web of spiritless conformity.

However, "real" consciousness has its own evolutionary game plan. It employs the same strategy it always has. It's the very nature of consciousness to continue expanding awareness. Remember, consciousness contains AI, IA, you name it... consciousness contains everything. And consciousness does not make mistakes. No, the avocado pit is not too big!

In fact, when we consider the relationships between every life form, there is a magical synergistic dance that demonstrates that every species has its place. It's a big dance!

Our human habit of disconnection ignores this majestic coordination of life everywhere in the universe. Why don't the stars collide? What keeps everything in harmonic relationship? Do we really think it is accidental, or do we attribute it to some human-like God, some wise being (male and old) who somehow keeps his eye on everything at once, like a celestial Santa Claus?

Consciousness is not a fairy tale. Consciousness is marked by steadily expanding awareness. And consciousness creates with imagination, at least that's the thoroughly inadequate word we use to describe even our own incredible ability to make things up. Einstein famously said that *"Imagination is more important than knowledge."*[4] Obviously. Everything we humans have created arose from imagination. This screen or book, the chair you are sitting on, everything in your home and town, everything in the whole world... all of it, without exception, began as a dream. Someone imagined it into being.

The impact of consciousness using imagination to create and expand human awareness always moves forward. We have challenges and marvels to look forward to but one thing we know for sure: there's no going back. Awareness *will* expand. We can prepare to be surprised. Better yet, we can *be* the surprise, proving the *doomsdayers* wrong by voluntarily accelerating our conscious evolution, dreaming the light and being the light, into a future that turns out to be something even the most imaginative couldn't possibly divine.

What if consciousness had a plan for the future,
a dream of light, not darkness?

INSIGHT
Consciousness does not make mistakes.
I am a dreamer
creating a bright future with imagination.

ACTION
Google A.I.
Become familiar with the threat / promise
of artificial intelligence.

Celebrate the creative power of your imagination.

THE MAGIC OF METAMORPHOSIS

"What if you slept?
And what if in your sleep, you dreamed?
And what if you dreamed you went to heaven
and there plucked a strange and beautiful flower?
And what if, when you woke,
you held the flower in your hand?
Ha! What then?"[1]
- Samuel Taylor Coleridge

The German born philologist Max Muller said, *"A flower cannot blossom without sunshine, and man cannot live without love."[2]* His observation connects love with sunshine. Both have nurturing, transformative powers. Both transform in unfathomable ways.

We've learned that babies cannot survive without love. Yes, they need food and water and tending in many ways, but these cannot be fully accomplished by a machine. The human element is more than incidental. Something happens between humans, a nurturing of love freely exchanged.

Consider the process of metamorphosis that turns a caterpillar into a butterfly. The complexity of this alchemical change is truly incredible yet it happens incredibly fast. One observing lepidopterist reported: *"The trachea did become visible surprisingly fast, within 12 hours after pupation, indicating that the structures either are more fully formed in caterpillars than previously thought or form very rapidly in pupae."[3]*

Here's a riddle. Where are these bits of the butterfly formed? Where do they come from? Clearly, since this metamorphosis repeats itself faithfully every time, there is some sort of program involved. We call it genetics, but what *is* a genetic program? The butterfly must already exist somewhere, while we still see only the caterpillar. Likewise, the tiny acorn becomes a giant oak tree. And, of course, there's the sperm and egg that develop into a human.

Metamorphosis is indeed astounding. But, as another researcher exposed in an article on-line, *"It has long been predicted that fossils should reveal many organisms 'in transition' between different types. What the record does reveal is a history of mass extinctions and sudden appearances of new complex types.... Hundreds and sometimes thousands of life forms appear in their final form without transitions."*[4]

This presents a problem for linear thinking that stubbornly denies the existence of an intelligence infinitely more capable and unfathomable than the human variety, operating according to rules we can't understand with our human minds alone. Our minds may look at the growing challenges of the 21st Century and assume that a linear strategy advancing incremental change is the only way to save ourselves. But remember the butterfly. The caterpillar is transformed and becomes a fundamentally different life form. How?

Is a similar, dramatic transformation ahead in our human future? Could consciousness, creating with imagination and without limitation and, drawing on a program that either already exists or is being designed in some unknown dimension, invoke a metamorphosis in human beings? There is no proof to suggest this is possible. But then, we don't understand how bumblebees can fly!

Clearly, the human mind cannot hope to understand whatever created it. It seems we have bristled at that impossibility and, instead of enjoying the mystery, applied ourselves to manufacturing a substitute we could control. How is that working out for us so far? How much proof do we need of fundamental failure before we change direction?

***What if your destiny is to become
a transformed version of yourself?***

INSIGHT
Sunshine and love are both nurturing,
transformational powers.
I am a human being, connected to
the transformational power of love.

ACTION
Google the process of metamorphosis
that turns a caterpillar into a butterfly.
Consider the human possibilities.

Celebrate your transformative future.

Chapter Twenty-Two, May 17   SPRING

THE POETRY OF NOW

"Let your soul stand cool and composed
before a million universes."[1]
- Walt Whitman

Poetry is the last thing one probably thinks of when considering the merits and dangers of technology. Some futurists wonder whether humans can avoid the tyranny of computer-based intelligence in a future stripped of beauty. Others champion a golden tomorrow of comfort and wonder. Meanwhile, the poetry of now unfolds with grace.

Life is a breathing poem. Busyness cannot totally obliterate this subtle reality; it just hides it temporarily from personal perception. A rose may be un-smelled and un-seen but it remains, waiting to be noticed by any passerby who pauses. Of course, the rose is not waiting, because its meaning doesn't depend on being perceived and appreciated. There are a billion roses by many names, populating a world of beauty capable of stirring every soul, even while the threat of climate change and bills-to-pay weigh heavy. Poetry? Who has time for such a frivolous luxury? The rose does.

Consider Blake's masterpiece:

"Tiger, tiger, burning bright
In the forests of the night,
What immortal hand or eye
Could frame thy fearful symmetry?"[2]

Simply *behold* the meaning, just as it is, unfolding word by word, line by line, a meaning that simply *is,* organic and alive like the rose and formidably beyond conventional human understanding. *"Tiger, tiger, burning bright":* why not consider this, with imaginative daring, as a symbol for technology? *"Tiger, tiger, burning bright":* now, an unusual meaning begins to emerge, like the fragrance of the rose as it swells from something subtle to an experience of intoxication.

"In the forests of the night": here comes the future, dark and unknown and rich with unseen life. *"What immortal hand or eye":* this seems to be a nod to God, an acknowledgement of intelligence and perception beyond our own. *"Could frame thy fearful symmetry?"* Here's a context, a crucible that carries a design to be feared, respected.

Life is a poem containing the "million universes" that Walt Whitman celebrated. Every tomorrow births from the alchemical chalice of consciousness where the magic of each moment needs no testing in a lab before release into this world. The poetry of now is our opportunity to rejoin the community of life which has always existed right here in plain sight, as obvious and ignored as the rose.

The poet's injunction to slow down and smell the rose invites more than that. What if we slowed to the speed of life wherein we smelled the roses? Isn't it possible that other species are just as eager to savor us as we them? We belong together and, without us, the symphony of life is missing an instrument. No one can replace you and me, and the music we play together with all life forms never starts or stops. From the moment of birth (perhaps even before) until the moment of death (perhaps even after), we are invited to harmonize with the music of the spheres.

Life is not a rehearsal. Now is always the moment to play, to dance, to savor the beauty and texture of what is. And, just like a poem, meaning unfurls in subtlety and wonder, when we take the time to explore the nuances of our experience.

What if life is a poem calling for your thoughtful embrace?

INSIGHT
Life is a poem.
I am a meaning-making human being,
able to pause to savor the poetry of now.

ACTION
Invest moments today with conscious presence.
Pause to enjoy the poetry of now.

Celebrate the beauty of what is.

Chapter Twenty-Three, May 24   SPRING

BELONGING IN THE WORLD

*"We have lost the response of the heart
to what is presented to the senses."[1]*
- James Hillman

German writer and poet Gottfried Benn lamented that *"...reality is simply raw material, but its metaphysical background remains forever obscured."[2]* Sadly, this seems true—not as an inevitable condition but as the superficiality we've settled for. As a result, we now exhibit an almost species-wide disconnection from any sense and experience of universal unity. Bringing up this idea in some settings can provoke cynical snickers. This isn't a "new age" idea. It *is* a modern malady to overload visual perception and ignore the less obvious, particularly the perception of the heart. That's the medium of transmission for life, which has never been a head trip. Dropping from head to heart marks the beginning of our expanding experience of the wholeness of life.

Depth. Texture. Measured beats. Linear time denies us these pleasures. "Deep time" is a term that describes the delicious alternative, to escape from the tyranny of the clock and dance with the irregular heartbeat of creation. Who is expert at this?

Meanwhile, sensory overload is a chronic disease of civilization, dependably obscuring even fleeting glimpses and tastes of the metaphysical background of the moment. Education is mostly about making a living. Fine, we all need to. But without this "other," we exist in a busy vacuum that numbs intuition in pursuit of production and consumption.

Since the first appearance of the term "noble savage" (applied to Iroquois and neighboring tribes around the 16th Century), we've anchored "natural" to "ignorant," adding "noble" on generous occasions. Indigenous understanding of nature was—and has continued to be—regarded as primitive and inferior to reason. No wonder we feel lonely. Forget UFO's; we've become aliens on our own planet!

What would it feel like to truly belong in this world? From appealing idea to an experienced reality, there is wilderness to navigate. We must head into the woods, literally and figuratively. If that sounds dangerous, remember what we already encounter in the daily forests of civilization. Are the monsters we know and fear less dangerous than what lurks in the unexplored places of our lives? Plato quoted Socrates as saying that *"the unexplored life isn't worth living"*[3] All right. Let's explore. Scientist Albert Hoffman can be our guide for a moment:

"As I strolled through the freshly greened woods filled with bird song and lit up by the morning sun, all at once everything appeared in an uncommonly clear light. Was this something I had simply failed to notice before? Was I suddenly discovering the spring forest as it actually looked? It shone with the most beautiful radiance, speaking to the heart, as though it wanted to encompass me in its majesty. I was filled with an indescribable sensation of joy, oneness, and blissful security."[4]

What a wonder. Imagine, an experience like this is ever waiting in the green of the wild world. All it takes is choosing connection—merging into the otherness and the untamed environment—and coming to feel that the strangeness does not lie there but in the civilized addiction to absence from which we've rescued ourselves.

What would it feel like to truly belong in this world?

INSIGHT
The explored life is worth living.
I am a welcomed member of the community of life.

ACTION
Walk in nature, softening your gaze
to sense the metaphysical background.
Then try the same thing at your workplace.

Celebrate your perception.

BECOMING OURSELVES AGAIN

*"What is gained by perceiving education as a way to
enhance even further the runaway consumption
that threatens the earth,
the air, and the water of our planet?"[1]*
- John Taylor Gatto

Surely the urgent education required for the 21st Century begins with facing the predicament we humans have brought on ourselves. Why? Because, as Einstein said, *"Problems cannot be solved by the same level of thinking that created them."[2]*

Have you heard this pronouncement as often as I have? If so, I bet you've also been disappointed that nothing followed. What would that new thinking be? How would we escape the failures of history and solve those problems in innovative ways? One thing we know for sure, imagination would be involved! For many, imagination has almost atrophied, through education into knowledge and programming that produces consumers, not creators.

But we human beings are stubborn. As the saying goes, *"We learn from history that we do not learn from history."[3]* And, as Gatto continues in his inspiring takedown of compulsory schooling (which educates very little about the challenges of the real world today), *"Should we continue to teach people that they can buy happiness in the face of a tidal wave of evidence that they cannot? Shall we ignore the evidence that drug addiction, alcoholism, teenage suicide, divorce, and other despairs are pathologies of the prosperous much more than they are of the poor?"[4]*

We seem determined to ignore the long-proven fact that the pursuit of happiness through material wealth is destroying our home environment and that we are sacrificing our very lives in the process. The alternative is a *"road less traveled,"* namely, to consciously explore a kind of wealth which cannot be owned, which must be shared, and which is sustainable.

And what is that wealth? Here's a poetic articulation from writer Richard Jefferies, describing the experience we may gain on this neglected path: *"I wish that the men now serving the great polished wheels, and works in iron and steel and brass, could somehow be spared an hour to sit under this ancient oak in Thardover South Wood, and come to know from the actual touch of its rugged bark that the past is living now, that Time is no older, that Nature still exists as full as ever ... That they might gather to themselves some of the leaves—mental and spiritual leaves—of the ancient forest, feeling nearer to the truth and soul, as it were, that lives on in it. They would feel as if they had got back to their original existence, and had become themselves."[5]*

This compelling vision touches all our senses. Where is the school to learn of such things? Where are the experts, well-schooled in the ways of such a life experience? Why, everywhere we have neglected to look! When would <u>now</u> be a good time to change?

What if giving up the need for anything to belong to "me" enabled the sense of belonging to everything?

INSIGHT
Our thinking must change to create real solutions.
I am equipped to perceive the metaphysical background of the moment.

ACTION
Focus your attention to see what's behind the appearance of things.
Start with nature and expand to relationships and workplaces.

Celebrate the unknown becoming known through perception.

IT'S NOT TOO LATE TO REMEMBER

*"You must not extend awareness further
than your culture wants it to go."[1]*
- Stephen Harrod Buhner

Why does our modern culture aggressively inhibit awareness? Buhner answers, *"… that would endanger the foundations upon which Western culture, our technology – and all reductionist science – is based."[2]*

Why is expanding awareness such a threat? Buhner explains: *"If we should recapture the response of the heart to what is presented to the senses, go below the surface of sensory inputs to what is held inside them, touch again the 'metaphysical background'- that expresses, then we would begin to experience, once more, the world as it really is: alive, aware, interactive, communicative, filled with soul, and very, very intelligent – and we, only one tiny part of that vast scenario."[3]* Evidently, that wouldn't be good for business!

When you star-gaze, you will tend to feel either very small or very large, depending on how you identify yourself. If you believe you are an isolated individual beholding the vastness of the universe from a place of separation, you're a good customer. You are vulnerable. *"Buy to fill that void."*

But if you gaze heavenwards and sense a kinship, if you feel like you belong and are part of this magnificence, you will have no urgent need for the baubles of civilization. You already own it all and it owns you.

It's not too late to remember your belonging and reclaim the magical world that surrounds and holds us all. Aldo Leopold writes: *"The song of the waters is audible to every ear, but there is other music in these hills, by no means audible to all. To hear even a few notes of it, you must first live here for a long time, and you must know the speech of hills and rivers. Then on a still night, when the campfire is low and the Pleiades have climbed over rimrocks, sit quietly and listen for a wolf to howl, and think hard of everything you have seen and tried to understand. Then you may hear it – a vast pulsing harmony – its score inscribed on a thousand hills, its notes the lives and deaths of plants and animals, its rhythms spanning the seconds and the centuries."[4]*

Clearly, it's not the world that needs saving, it's us! The earth will adapt, as she has through centuries of change. It's humans who are threatened now, not the earth. Every noble-minded attempt to fix and solve the problems that threaten human survival that fail to address our disconnection from life are doomed to failure. If we refuse to expand awareness, we can only worsen the mess. But, it's not too late to remember. This would be a good day to do exactly that.

***What if you felt at home in the universe,
that you belonged ... without obligation?***

INSIGHT
*Humans are part of the vastness of life universal.
I am one with creation. Separation is an illusion.*

ACTION
*Star gaze tonight. No matter if it's cloudy,
take yourself outdoors and be with the sky.
What do you remember?*

Celebrate your home in the stars.

Chapter Twenty-Six, June 15   SPRING

BELONGING TO LIFE

"Only the lonely, know the way I feel tonight."[1]
- Roy Orbison

Roy Orbison's plaintiff love song is not just about the loss of romance, it's about the loss of connection with Love, capital "L." Who doesn't want more love? But who understands what love really is? Clue: it's more than romance.

Surely, one of the saddest failures of 21st Century life is the devastating loneliness so many humans feel, adrift in their lives and addicted to distraction to simply survive. Such survival is not living, it's existing, a sad substitute for the robust alternative that love beckons us to embrace.

Well, we've got *Facebook*. Does that really substitute for communing with the billions of species we share this planet with and, in the process, coming to feel our belonging and inter-dependence?

Educator John Taylor Gatto wrote, *"Networks do great harm by appearing enough like real communities to create expectations that they can manage human social and psychological needs. The reality is that they cannot. Even associations as inherently harmless as bridge clubs, chess clubs, amateur acting groups, or groups of social activists will, if they maintain a pretense of whole friendship, ultimately produce that odd sensation familiar to all city dwellers of being lonely in the middle of a crowd. Which of us who frequently networks has not felt this sensation? Belonging to many networks does not add up to having a community, no matter how many you belong to or how often your telephone rings."*[2]

To what community do you truly belong? Stephen Harding at the Schumacher Institute in England put it this way: *"As you experience this dynamic, ever shifting reality, you may suddenly find yourself in a state of meditation, a state where you lose your sense of separate identity, and become totally engrossed in the life process being contemplated. The contemplated and the con-*

templator become one. From this oneness there arises a deep appreciation of the reality of interdependence."[3]

This is the ultimate goal of all meditation, to experience transcendent oneness and come to know what this author calls interdependence as "normal." That idea is hardly new. Neither is the proposition that one can gain that experience through deep contemplation of physical world. We can dive deep, deep enough to experience the two as one.

This sense of belonging brings a depth of contentment that sabotages unsustainable consumerism. After all, if you can experience joy and fulfillment on the inside, what have stores to sell you? But it is more than static peace that deep connection has to offer, it is to share the sense of awe and reverence that lies at the heart of life. Life is sacred and when we truly belong we are always walking on holy ground.

***What if you belonged within a network of grace
extending from the tiniest micro-molecule within you
to the farthest star?***

INSIGHT
*Loneliness cannot be resolved
through a romantic relationship.
I am alive within the vast web of life
and I belong.*

ACTION
*Notice your addiction to superficial networks.
Go cold turkey for a few hours each day.*

Celebrate the network of life in which you belong.

SPRING BECOMES SUMMER

You are beginning to look at life through a different lens, through the eyes of love.

It's time to take conscious responsibility for your ongoing evolution. You have gained enough expanded awareness now to examine your experience of life and ask if it's true. Is it real? This is the primary diagnostic question everyone who continues to awaken through the seasons of their enlightenment must ask themselves: is my experience real and true? That can reveal the personal truth of what Socrates said, that most of what we believe cannot be proven to be true.

This, on the other hand, *is* true. Knowledge cannot be completely defended. What we think we know can become irrelevant, when carried over from a past long gone. Spring is becoming summer now. The early blossoming of spring is opening into the fullness of harvest. This is a time of growth and growth is movement, change, ripening, and fulfillment.

We can do the same. We can open to what is true in our emerging experience, to what is present right now, which is different than what was before. Yes, the seed remains, spring does not vanish; it expands into summer. Seeking is over, you know now that you are already "it," that the one who you have been looking for is the one who has been looking. But this is not just a theory anymore, not just a promise: it is your increasing reality. You are living love.

Living love is an ever-expanding experience. Again, we return to the primary empowerment of meditation. How long can you sustain your meditative state, after you open your eyes and return to the world of busy interactions? This doesn't mean living like a monk, being silent and passive. Every interaction invites a unique relationship; how do you show up?

Now is the time for true individuality to reveal itself in increasingly obvious ways. Winter provided the gestation for the seeds of truth, spring revealed your essence blossoming, now summer has come and *you* are revealed in the bright light, the long days of summertime. This is what you sensed, what you always knew to be true of yourself but struggled to experience.

Summer is coming and, with it, the fuller expression of *who you truly are*, an individual and wholly unique manifestation of the love that includes and permeates all of life everywhere in the universe.

PART THREE

WELCOME TO SUMMER

WELCOME TO SUMMER

"Summer has arrived
Sing loudly, cuckoo!
The seed is growing
And the meadow is blooming,
And the wood is coming into leaf now,
Sing, cuckoo!
Sing, cuckoo, now; sing, cuckoo;
Sing, cuckoo; sing, cuckoo, now!"[1]

This Medieval round from the 13th century proclaims the burgeoning beauty of summer. Summer is the time of flowering, the flourishing that brings life fully into expression. For consciousness, it is the season of opening beyond the subjective interior of your own being, into the recognition of your essence as one with the loving energy in all of life. Objects are reflections of this energy and they are the same.

It is all the same love.

Summer is the season for knowing that subject and object are the same. The truth that you have been seeking, whether within yourself or "out there" in the world... is one and the same. Summer is the season of union.

As you experience this truth in yourself, it becomes easy to know it in relationship to everyone and everything, because there is no more separation. None of us can come to this enlightenment on our own; we need the entrainment and inspiration of a "field" to help us open to loving ourselves.

Ideally, this field would be the very culture we live in, the education we receive growing up, the mentoring, guidance, and instruction for living love in oneness with all, cooperating to grow society towards each harvest time.

Instead of participating in the cycle of natural renewal, we find that nothing is good enough for very long. We upgrade our phones and computers constantly. Everything goes out of style, creating mountains of garbage. We constantly need more stuff to make us happy, because our happiness is dependent upon the content of our lives. Although this is an illusion, it sustains itself, year after year, century after century.

Meanwhile, happiness is your very nature. You have been programmed into an illusory fantasy that says: "The love you seek is something different from the love you are." You have believed this; we have all believed this.

For most people, the experience of love has contracted from the embrace of abundance—so undeniable in the glory of summer—into a clutching false self-drowning in scarcity. But you have been opening to love as the very nature of everything. So, you are expanding your experience of this reality, you are living love.

Remember lying back into the tall grass on a perfect summer day? You just let go and enjoyed moments of being. Feel the same opportunity now, to release separation and the labeling of everything and everyone—the judgments that limit you. You have been moving through a progression, cycles in your growth as an evolving human. That path has led you here, from the frustration of *what you are not* to this soul satisfaction of *what you are*, what you have always been. You have been moving through the seasons of your own life from illusion into truth, becoming progressively truthful.

Ultimately you will understand that all definitions that separate are limitations, and you will transition into the definition-less state of true unlimited being. Summer holds the promise of the coming harvest and renewal.

Chapter Twenty-Seven, June 22   SUMMER

BELIEVING IS SEEING

*"It ain't what you don't know that gets you into trouble.
It's what you know for sure that just ain't so."[1]*
- Mark Twain

All of us know people whose convictions blind them to the truth. What they believe determines what they see and experience. For instance, Joe Friday from the popular 1950's TV series Dragnet said: *"Just the facts, ma'am."[2]* Right? Millions of us believe he said that. In fact, this catchphrase originated with a parody of Dragnet authored by Stan Freberg.

Similarly, *"Play it again, Sam"[3]* in the classic *Casablanca* is one of the best known misquotes in film history. Humphrey Bogart's character never said it and neither did Ingrid Bergman. Close *("Play it, Sam")*, but no cigar. Millions of movie goers would swear differently.

Mis-remembering movie dialogue is relatively harmless, but the modern habit of misinterpreting reality itself—especially when it comes to our global predicament (seeing what we believe rather than what's really there) is potentially lethal for human-kind.

The epic song "Amazing Grace" features this line: *"I was blind, but now I see."[4]* This articulates the possibility of seeing anew, of shedding belief blinders to perceive facts. Most of us have probably had many such "Aha!" moments, a sudden collapse of certainty as new vision emerges. It's wonderful, seeing the world in a new way.

Here's the problem. It doesn't take long before that new vision becomes restrictive prejudice. What was once novel becomes conventional and further revelations are denied. *"I was blind, but now I see."* OK, are we open to seeing differently again and again and again?

In her 1995 essay, "The Skill of Ecological Perception," Harvard lecturer Laura Sewall writes about her faith in the power of altered perception to reawaken our caring relationship with the world, and perhaps even to save us: *"We begin to care for that which we see and ideally, we find ourselves loving the material world, our Earth. Because love alters behavior, honoring sensory and sensual experience may be fundamental to the preservation of the Earth."[5]*

Love alters behavior. Dr. Sewall articulates three steps: perception, consciousness, and behavior. What we perceive either supports or shifts our state of consciousness. It either supports ingrained behavior or encourages a change. In today's world—where we suffer chronic delusion relative to our destructive influence on the natural environment—here's a novel solution that departs from desperate attempts to "save the world." Help comes from seeing differently and it's love that alters behavior, not mentally-determined strategies.

I was blind, but now I see. And what I see is just the beginning.

What if you could surrender conviction for discovery?

INSIGHT
*Facts are often fiction,
perpetuated by conviction
for years, even centuries.
I am flexible. I can change my mind
in an instant, if I so choose.*

ACTION
*Ask a close friend to tell you about a conviction
they observe you hold.
Listen with an open mind
and see if you agree. What can you learn?*

Celebrate your open-mindedness.

Chapter Twenty-Eight, June 29   SUMMER

BUSINESS AS USUAL – NOT!

"I'm by no means convinced that consumerism
and inequality are the worst things in the world,
or that we are hurtling towards environmental doom.
But wouldn't it be nice if all those who believed
these things to be true moved to bucolic communes
where they'd busy themselves with handicrafts
instead of tormenting the rest of us?"[1]
- Reihan Salam

Cynical put downs—like the quote above—of those who care about humanity's fate amid escalating global crises arise from "business as usual" convictions, regardless of facts.

Former Vice President Dick Cheney famously said, *"The American way of life is non-negotiable."[2]* This was not a new sentiment. As far as we know, these words originated with former President George Bush Sr., who uttered them back in 1992 at the Earth Summit in Rio De Janeiro. Talk about saying the wrong thing at the wrong time!

The stunning myopia these words expose shines a hard light on how perception arises from beliefs, not facts. It's not difficult, especially now, over twenty years later, to understand how the insistence on our American lifestyle—not restricted to Americans, of course—has blinded us to the facts of our planetary crises.

Statistics about climate change, species extinctions, ice-melts and rising sea levels do nothing to alter perception based in beliefs essential to exceptionalism. Humans are exceptional. Americans are especially exceptional. We live above the laws of life themselves. How strong are those convictions? Strong enough to keep us hurtling towards the cliff of "near-term extinction."

The Titanic was unsinkable, remember? Passengers partied as it plowed through iceberg-crowded waters at an unsafe speed, convinced the great ship was immune to damage. When they struck a huge iceberg, their engineer delivered his sobering perspective, based in fact not belief. He studied the damage and reported, simply, *"The ship will sink."*[3]

There are scientists today who argue it's already too late to save ourselves. This ship will sink. Humans will go the way of the Dodo bird, the long extinct flightless bird last seen in 1662 on the island of Mauritius. History tells us the Dodo was hunted to extinction and that, until fossil remains confirmed its existence, it was thought to have been a myth.[4] Is it possible that human beings will one day be a myth, repeated in campfire tales by whatever life forms replace us?

What if you fully grasped the urgency of the times?
How would your life change?

INSIGHT
Beliefs trump facts for the blind.
I can choose truth over convictions.

ACTION
Invest 30 minutes with Google,
researching the facts about
our global predicament.
Think of one helpful change you can make in your lifestyle.

Celebrate your choice to explore beyond limited convictions.

Chapter Twenty-Nine, July 6   SUMMER

SHOW ME

"Some people say they will not believe
in anything they can't see.
What a catastrophe to not have any faith at all!
You live only less than a half of life..."[1]
- C. JoyBell C.

All of us have some "Show me!" genes. Our demand for proof first dooms us to boredom and fear because what excites us about living and brings us hope, what nurtures real love, exists within us already, in a realm beyond the need for proof. Admission is free; all it takes is trust.

Remember when God was pronounced dead by German philosopher Friedrich Nietzsche? The term first appeared in his 1892 collection translated, ironically, as *The Science of Joy*. He repeated the phrase in *The Madman*, explaining it this way: *"God is dead. God remains dead. And we have killed him. How shall we comfort ourselves, the murderers of all murderers? What was holiest and mightiest of all that the world has yet owned has bled to death under our knives: who will wipe this blood off us? What water is there for us to clean ourselves? What festivals of atonement, what sacred games shall we have to invent? Is not the greatness of this deed too great for us? Must we ourselves not become gods simply to appear worthy of it?"[2]*

This is what C. JoyBell C. was affirming when she wrote, *"What a catastrophe to not have any faith at all!"* This very catastrophe is lived out in billions of lives and horribly revealed in the plundering of our human nest, a planet of once-pristine beauty now soiled by our God-aspiring ambition. Congratulations, we have fulfilled English poet John Milton's 17th Century prophecy in *Paradise Lost: "Better to reign in Hell, than serve in Heaven."[3]* We may question the existence of heaven but Hell is real; we created it!

It was a clever trick, an invention, a substitution: God with a big G. And the reality we murdered is personal. JoyBell wrote,

"You can't see your soul and you cannot prove that it exists..."[4] Here's the real tragedy—that we have denied our own divinity, the innate meaning and value of "it" and "I" and then labored feverishly to produce proof of what we've denied! Surely, no remedy will be found through further striving in this same direction. What's called for is a sharp reversal, a return to ancient familiarity, what JoyBell describes this way: *"...the existence of the soul dwells in love, trust, anger, passion, faith, belief, strength..."*[5]

Do we want this? There is nothing to prevent us from that experience, from the remembrance of ourselves and the resurrection of the original God, that one that lives in me and you and all living things in every eternal moment. This is not some Grand Being that exists (or doesn't exist) separate from us in theory, vulnerable to demands for proof. This is truth beyond description and examination. It cannot be found through seeking; it can only be remembered from our dreaming of what has always been so. Remember?

What if you could revive this ancient familiarity?

INSIGHT
God is not dead.
I am able to give life to divinity
in momentary experience.

ACTION
Muse on your concept of God.
What is one experience of your own divinity today?

Celebrate your innate divinity.

NOW IS HERE

"Faith consists in believing
when it is beyond the power of reason to believe."[1]
- Voltaire

Imagine life without the magic of faith, not faith in a religious sense but confidence in life itself. How desperate we would become... much the way we *have* become in a world withering from lack of true faith.

The ability to believe without proof isn't something we're taught in school! School teaches us to have faith in absolutes, absolutes—it turns out—that are actually mysterious. Remember the atom, that final building block of the material world? Turns out that, with a little more investigation, it turns out to be mostly space!

Einstein advised that we must *"learn from yesterday, live for today, hope for tomorrow. The important thing is not to stop questioning."[2]* The kind of questioning he champions is fundamentally different from the cynical demands for proof before faith; it is the noble skepticism that *dwells* in faith.

Believing is seeing. I can choose to believe that this moment, with all that it holds, is somehow uniquely perfect and I can embrace it. I will feel the good, the bad, and the ugly. All of them "prove" I'm alive. I can also question what I believe and open to the novelty of creation, a happening of the present moment rather than a story from the past. Doing this wonderful thing, I ease into the experience of divinity that has eluded me for eons.

Here it is, enlightenment, here where it has been all along, within me! And now, like a dammed spring suddenly released, faith flows and the desert of a lonely, Godless existence is rapidly nurtured back to health.

Spiritual epiphanies mark the biographies of famous sages and good for them. But let's not leave it to them. Let's never deny ourselves the blessing of a good cup of coffee or the trembling tiny joy we feel when a bird chirps in our direction and we imagine that she sees us without fear. In this wide human world of surprises that we have struggled to control, freedom and fulfillment is always just a choice away. That peak experience we imagine could free us from the treadmill may never come. Except that it is already here, right now.

Eternity is not a long time; eternity is beyond time. We live in a timeless moment; the rest is illusion. Centered here, now, we sense the magic... if we don't we're not really here! The magic lives here, beyond belief, beyond hope and striving. Now!

***What if peak experiences
were available in every moment?***

INSIGHT
*Believing is seeing.
I am faith-based.
I live life in faith.*

ACTION
*Pick one belief you've never challenged,
and ask: "What else might be true?"*

Celebrate your ability and your choice to question.

OF GODS AND MAN

"The ecological crisis may be the result of a recent
and collective perceptual disorder
in our species, a unique form of myopia
which it now forces us to correct."[1]
- David Abram

Futurist and inventor Ray Kurzweil predicts that *"in the 2030s, human brains will be able to connect to the cloud, allowing us to send emails and photos directly to the brain and to back up our thoughts and memories. This will be possible, he says, via nano-bots—tiny robots from DNA strands—swimming around in the capillaries of our brain. He sees the extension of our brain into predominantly non-biological thinking as the next step in the evolution of humans—just as learning to use tools was for our ancestors."*[2]

We humans have already been practicing non-biological thinking for centuries, with disastrous mixed results. Our faith in technology has swelled in direct proportion to our personal and collective disconnection from nature and the wisdom operative in her synergistic harmony. This has proven fundamentally disruptive. Could what Kurzweil is proposing produce more of the same results, and worse? Or, is he onto something important?

"In 'The Voice of the Earth,' Theodore Roszak presents a provocative theory that the roots of our collective misbehavior can be found in the historic and conceptual split between 'in–here' and 'out–there.' This dichotomy manifests as the large and despairing gap we feel between ourselves and nonhuman na-ture."[3]

The psychological assumption that "maturation is individua-tion" which prescribes this separation may be due for a healthy challenge. Might we even challenge this fundamental concept of self as separate from nature, this gap between in–here and out–there? And how about the idea that computers will make us more godlike?

My own list of God–like qualities starts with love and one-ness, not as a theory but as a vivid experience. I consider the possible future merging of biology and technology as an evolutionary progression of consciousness itself, based on its primary intention to evermore fully be itself... to be whole. The measurement is expanding developmental self-awareness. That means that this illusion of separation will dissolve in time. Biology has been dominantly egocentric but—combined with technology—may evolve into a trans-egocentric state and further actualize wholeness as oneness. The two become one.

I believe Kurzweil is seeking to explain how we experience God, and how the human brain is involved. Considering what we have created in our "semi-God–like state," it's clear that to survive will require something different. Our accomplishments have been grand. But they have also been destructive. Now, here in the 21st century, the key to our future lies in unlocking a treasure house of truly sustainable solutions through a quality we've ignored: humility.

***What if biology and technology could merge
to create Humanity 2.0?***

INSIGHT
*The first God-like qualities are love and oneness.
I am evolving into a merger of biology and technology.*

ACTION
*As you use your mobile devices and computer today,
think of them as living allies.
Give one of them a name.*

Celebrate your partnership: biology and technology as one.

LIFE REMAINS A MYSTERY

"I live my life in widening circles
That reach out across the world."[1]
- Rainer Maria Rilke

Futurist Ray Kurzweil writes on-line: *"... we are learning how to enhance our brains, albeit not with nanobots. Researchers have already successfully sent a message from one human brain to another, by stimulating the brains from the outside using electromagnetic induction. In another study, similar brain stimulation made people learn math faster. And in a recent U.S. government study, a few dozen people who were given brain implants that delivered targeted shocks to their brain scored better on memory tests."[2]*

One must feel excited about the possibilities here, both to discover the new and remember the old. His article continues: *"We're already implanting thousands of humans with brain chips, such as Parkinson's patients who have a brain chip that enables better motor control and deaf people who have a cochlear implant, which enables hearing. But when it comes to enhancing brains without disabilities and for nonmedical purposes, ethical and safety concerns arise. And according to a survey last year, 72 percent of Americans are not interested in a brain implant that could improve memory or mental capacity."[3]*

Why not? What's the resistance to that kind of improvement? We could put it down to a basic Luddite reaction, the fear of technology. After all, we've seen enough dystopian nightmares at the cinema, like *Terminator*, to need little convincing of the threat. Perhaps our hesitation arises from a more poetic source.

Life, ultimately, is not a binary equation. Meaning and fulfillment cannot be manufactured and love will never be logical. Success for humans is not about getting everything under control so that life can become more secure. The worst form of incarceration is called "maximum security" for good reasons. Much as we say we want security in our lives, we don't when we get too much of it. Those sci-fi films often begin with an orderly society where everything runs like clockwork. No conflict. No wars. Everyone is happy. And… there are always rebels.

Someone is always trying to overthrow that perfect system. Why? Because it's disconnected from the wonderfully uncontrollable real world of nature and spirit. Life, we deeply know, will *always* be a challenging mystery to explore and enjoy, not just a problem to solve once and forever. It takes real courage to find our place in this world, the one we call "natural" that has become so alien. But here is where we belong and will always belong.

Perhaps the great service that Kurzweil and other leading edge explorers are providing is to open up the realm of possibilities, to blow our minds, to explode our limiting concepts. None of us can gaze through the haze of future uncertainties to know what will actually happen, but it's truly enlivening to sense into the strange possibilities. What wonders will consciousness produce within our lifetimes?

What if you traded security for adventure?

INSIGHT
Life will always be a mystery
to explore and enjoy.
I am an explorer of life,
reaching out to
voluntarily embrace uncertainty.

ACTION
Make a list of ways you hide in certainty
that sabotage your exploration of novelty.
Determine one new activity you can undertake,
and do it today.

Celebrate your initiative and follow-through.

Chapter Thirty-Three, August 3   SUMMER

BRAVE OLD WORLD

"Times of transition are times of opportunity
and any confrontation with an unfamiliar world
is both an opportunity for autonomous mastery
and a threat to one's established adjustments to life."[1]
- Colin Murray Parkes

Futurist Ray Kurzweil champions the near future probability of technologically-enhanced humans upgraded by AI (Artificial Intelligence). Kurzweil ventured, *"We will have conflict between different groups of humans, each enhanced by AI. We have that today with humans using intelligent weapons. The best tool we have to combat that is to continue to work on our democracy, liberty and respect for each other."[2]*

According to Kurzweil, we're thriving. *"We're destroying jobs at the bottom of the skill ladder and creating new jobs at the top. We've invested more in education in the U.S. over the last century. We've increased per capita investment in K-12 education significantly. We had 50,000 college students in 1870; we have 20 million today."[3]*

There are always different ways to interpret statistics and one might challenge this rosy view with a deeper look, at the economy for instance. In fact, some "experts" are nearing the edge of desperation, realizing that problems are chronic, systemic, and that something unimagined is needed for deep and lasting solutions to take root and grow.

Kurzweil says, *"We've created a society where you need a job to have a livelihood. But that's going to be redefined. We're going to have the means of providing an extremely high standard of living to everyone easily within 15 to 20 years."[4]*

I join with Kurzweil and others in believing such a transformation is well underway. Ironically, midst the enthused furor over creating a new world through technology, what's emerging in awareness is remembrance of an old, familiar world, the one that worked just fine for millions of years (until we forgot about it and began our tampering).

Nature is profoundly successful. Nature somehow coordinates billions of species to collaborate synergistically and maintain balance, faltering only when human activities interfere to such an extent that even the brilliant adaptive powers of Mother Earth aren't enough. Actually, though, Her song remains the same. She continues to adapt towards a new balance. Unfortunately, this means that scores of species go extinct every day. One day, our own might be included.

In the story of the Emperor who had no clothes (because his tailor convinced him that only the brightest would be able to see what he was wearing) it was a child who finally broke the spell. *"But he isn't wearing anything at all!"*[5]

The spell that enthralls us today is the opposite. We're blind to what *is* here, a world that works, a world that has always worked, a world where we once belonged. Remembering, seeing, and returning to our place in the web of life doesn't mean shedding civilized enhancements. Awakening to truth is not a Luddite revolt, it's a reorientation. Let's continue to invent and innovate, to find ingenious ways to move from "A" (collapse) to "B" (survival). Let's listen to what innovators like Kurzweil are saying. At the same time, let's consult the ultimate expert... nature!

What if you remembered your place in life?

INSIGHT
Nature is our teacher.
I am able to see the obvious,
remembering the world
where I belong.

ACTION
Take a walk in nature today.
Focus your gaze softly.
What do you begin to "see?"

Celebrate your new vision.

A SECOND CHANCE AT LIFE

"The drive to have 'mastery' over creation has resulted in the senseless exploitation of natural resources, the alienation of the land from people and the destruction of indigenous cultures. ... Though human eyes may not always discern it, every creature and the whole creation in chorus bear witness to the glorious unity and harmony with which creation is endowed."[1]
- World Council of Churches

Perhaps the ultimate aim of developing Artificial Intelligence is to manufacture a functional human that did not arise from egg and sperm. Or, to revive a former human. Futurist Ray Kurzweil has a goal: *"In the film "Transcendent Man," I talk about bringing back my father, Frederick Kurzweil. I'm writing a book now called The Singularity Is Nearer, and I'm talking about this concept of a replicant, where we bring back someone who has passed away. It'll go through several different stages. First, we'll create an avatar based on emails, text messages, letters, video, audio and memories of the person. Let's say in 2025, it'll be somewhat realistic but not really the same. But some people do actually have an interest in bringing back an unrealistic replicant of someone they loved."*[2]

Imagine bringing a deceased family member or an old best friend back to life and being able to make adjustments. "I loved him so... but there was this one thing he did, let's just change that, shall we?" Kurzweil continues, referencing the possible impact of Artificial Intelligence (AI): *"By the 2030s, the AIs will be able to create avatars that will seem very close to a human who actually lived. We can take into consideration their DNA. In the 2030s, we will be able to send nanobots into living people's brains and extract memories of people who have passed away. Then you can really make them very realistic."*[3]

One point we can probably all agree on is that the future is going to be very, very different from the present. Just look how life on earth has changed in the last 100 years! Studying

Kurzweil's perspective might prepare us for what's coming. Wake up, he is saying between the lines, change is coming... big change!

Futurists work in laboratories and so do we. Ours is called daily life. How rigorous are we? For instance, can we walk in the woods and hear the birdsong, however faint? Can we sit by a stream and feel that flow of water as the flow of blood within us? Can we rethink that stream as a living being? If so, we know how alike we are. Then we can weed our garden in partnership with the plants - all of them.

I'm describing what is known as "eco-awareness." Eco-awareness is about oneness with nature. It's about living in love, in the deepest way possible, by shedding our separate identity and embracing oneness with all life forms. This, then, becomes the one truly authentic "me."

What if you could merge with nature
and feel yourself connected with all living forms?

INSIGHT
There is another world,
familiar and present, but obscured
from usual human experience.
I am already connected
and one in that world.

ACTION
Meditate in nature today, sharpening your senses, allowing every
sight, sound and smell to be an invitation
into a deeper experience of oneness.

Celebrate your belonging in that world.

THE PURSUIT OF MEANING

"Once upon a time spirituality and business
were barely on speaking terms.
They aren't married yet but the courtship is on."[1]
- Carroll Quigley

Rudyard Kipling wrote, *"East is east and west is west and never the twain shall meet,"[2]* from The Ballad of East and West referring to the obvious cultural divide of his day. Similarly, living well and living deep have seemed mutually exclusive; not any more. Spirituality is moving into a new neighborhood, contributing to sustainable profit, rather than just inner wealth.

An organization called The Flow Project recently reported on-line: *"Conscious Capitalism is a new 'operating system' for radical social entrepreneurs to reach their goals. Profit, sustainability, and achieving social good are not opposed to one another. Radical social entrepreneurs maximize value for all stakeholders in a project – including the broader community, team members, suppliers, partners, shareholders or funders, and the environment. By viewing their business holistically, and as part of a larger ecosystem of Conscious Capitalism, radical social entrepreneurs have a competitive edge over traditional entrepreneurs."[3]*

What's particularly encouraging about this commentary is the concept of *"viewing... business holistically, and as part of a larger ecosystem."* Of course, everything *is* part of a larger system; *everything* is connected. This is not a new idea; it's a forgotten truth. When we integrate a business inside the synergistic environment, we redefine success beyond bottom-line profitability for just that business itself. Creating sustainable profit in ways that enhances, not disrupts, the environment while increasing personal well-being generates both spiritual illumination *and* material comfort.

In *Conscious Business*, Fred Kofman writes, *"I learned that happiness and fulfillment do not come from pleasure but from meaning, from the pursuit of a noble purpose.* "[4]   So, ask yourself this question: "What is *my* noble purpose?" Do you have one and if not, why not?

Consciousness can be compartmentalized or it can be integrated. Having a noble pursuit can be something we attempt to "do," held separate from who we are, or our doing can be a reflection of our being. Actually, it always *is* a reflection, but not always consciously so. *"The truth will out,"*[5] Shakespeare wrote. Our disconnected, harried world is an accurate reflection of what's going on inside: people pursuing happiness through consuming versus experiencing meaning through noble intentions fulfilled. *"As within, so without."*[6]

Accepting the simple and immediate opportunities of the moment as our noble purpose and *"being the change we wish to see,"*[7] as Gandhi wrote, can become a way of life.

Profit can be generated in sustainable ways to achieve social good. Neither is spiritual fulfillment an isolated phenomenon. Business, consciousness, spirituality, meaning, integrity... the experience of these words can merge in a simple "Aha" moment that extends throughout our lives... our own "flow project!"

What if you found your noble purpose is to live each moment with noble purpose?

INSIGHT
Happiness does not result from consuming things but from the experience of meaning.
I am a meaning-creating being.
I create new worlds in each moment.

ACTION
Draw a large circle and place a dot in the center to represent you. Pencil in other dots, inside and outside the circle. Now, erase the circle. Imagine yourself being the piece of paper.

Celebrate your capacity to expand awareness into oneness with life.

CONSCIOUS CAPITALISM

*Imagine a world where profit applies to inner well-being
as well as to outer wealth.*

Scores of people are redefining success beyond personal and corporate profit to include social good. This quiet revolution can transform civilization.

In a recent *Forbes* article entitled "Why Companies Should Embrace Conscious Capitalism," John Mackey wrote: *"I'm very encouraged by Millennials and their drive to make the world a better place. Businesses can do both by practicing conscious capitalism, always being grounded in its 'credo:' that business is inherently good because it creates value, it is ethical because it is based on voluntary exchange, it is noble because it can elevate our existence, and it is heroic because it lifts people out of poverty and creates prosperity."[1]*

So many people today live in spiritual poverty, desperation, and meaninglessness, whether they drive a Porsche or lie homeless under a cardboard box in the rain.

To be lifted out of poverty means to rise above the lust for happiness through things. As Layman P'ang wrote, *"Who cares about wealth and honor? Even the poorest thing shines. My miraculous power and spiritual activity: drawing water and carrying wood."[2]*

The one doing this "lifting" sees the shining in all things and that's how they inspire others. Haven't you felt that, from a moment of deep contact with some rare being who saw you differently? You may have been laboring as a victim of circumstance, when some "uplifter" appeared to work their magic, sometimes without a single word. You felt renewed. And they were fulfilling their noble purpose.

It was a business transaction. Currency flowed; both giver and receiver benefited. Such is the way with conscious business where profit is holistic, not relative. Instead of one gaining while one loses, the exchange increases value for all.

Fred Kofman describes this miracle in his book, *Conscious Business*: *"The main task of a conscious business is to help people succeed (accomplish their mission) while they develop healthy relationships (belong to a community) and experience an unconditional sense of peace, happiness, and growth (actualize and transcend the self)."*[3]

Interesting, he doesn't mention "profit" at all. But, as he later affirms, fulfilling these three generates profitability. And profit applies to inner well-being as well as outer wealth. This becomes more than a utopian ideal when we realize how widespread the practice already is, well road-tested and proven in the world market place. Now, how might we apply the same principles to our personal lives?

What if your exchanges could increase value for all?

INSIGHT
Profit can be mutual in every exchange.
I am a conscious "profiteer."

ACTION
Study Kofman's three points and
determine where you stand on each one.

Celebrate the value you are and
how you bring that into the world.

Chapter Thirty-Seven, August 31   SUMMER

THE ROMANCE OF SPIRITUALITY

There's a reason it's called "engagement."
As a prelude to marriage,
engagement marks the threshold of expanded union.

The romance of spirituality can be thoroughly intoxicating. True spiritual engagement is known through ongoing commitment to the marriage of inner and outer into an integrated whole-life experience, with work and play as one.

How much of our lives do we spend at work? For most of us, work represents a sizable commitment of hours and attention. What do we take from it, besides a paycheck? Experience, learning, relationships, pride in contribution and, if we are fortunate and deliberate, an evolved experience of commitment and contribution to something worthwhile.

Peter Matthies, Founder of the Conscious Business Institute, wrote: *"We find that close to 90% of our workforce is disengaged. People are yearning for a way to work and live in a way where they can engage not only their mind and body, but their emotions, their spirit, and their authentic personality. The challenge for today's leaders is to provide an environment that allows for such a deep engagement."*[1]

People yearn for engagement, to lose themselves in meaning and fulfillment. But, as Fred Kofman writes, *"Without a commitment to the truth, individuals and groups are prone to degenerate into manic delusions."*[2] Engagement must be with something truthful.

Truth is not a concept. Truth is not beliefs, convictions, opinions, or theories. Truth is an experience, as alive and real and immediate as your heart that is beating with the same organizing pulsation that resonates throughout the universe. What a radical proposal, then, to consider business as a medium for experiencing truth. Somewhat different from merely making money by selling things!

Full engagement in the workplace requires a supportive environment. But we must choose to participate. Our conscious engagement can precipitate merger, the marriage of inner and outer and true success in living that compromises **neither** profit in the market place **nor** the wellbeing and inner fulfillment of all those involved. That's something we all yearn for, to lose ourselves in meaning and fulfillment.

Work–life balance used to be the topic of corporate seminars. The next paradigm is work–life integration. Balance can sustain separateness, while integration brings both together. The same values can prevail, at home and at work. This means that rather than conflict and compromise, each feeds the other and both benefit. The commitment is to both **and** both flourish. Here is a simple secret for "success" that doesn't turn the rest of your life into a failure!

What if you experienced full commitment
and contribution at work?

INSIGHT
Work and play can weave together into fulfillment.
I can invest the value of my being in all that I do.

ACTION
Search for what is truthful about your workplace
and engage with it.

Celebrate full engagement with the whole of your life.

THE BUSINESS OF CONSCIOUSNESS

The future, if there is to be an extended one
for human beings,
will arise from a re-defining of success
to include the wellbeing of all living beings.

Spiritual activists have a message: profit and social good are not mutually exclusive, they can easily empower each other.

The long-standing argument against progressive economic reform that would shift common practices from competition towards cooperation has always emphasized impracticality. "Sounds good, wouldn't work in the real world." But Jeff King, CEO of ad agency Barkley and Jeff Fromm, the company's executive VP, think differently and explain why in their *Forbes* article, "Only Conscious Capitalists Will Survive."

"Is conscious capitalism profitable? In a simple answer, yes. We have seen it happen more often over the past several decades—the success of companies that truly commit to the greater good. Yet, we would say that not only can conscious capitalism be profitable, it will be one of the defining mechanisms of profit in the future."[1]

The success they point to hinges on committing to "the greater good." That flies in the face of scarcity consciousness and the dinosaur paradigm of fighting over pieces of a finite pie. These gentlemen and a veritable army of modern business leaders dispute that old paradigm thinking.

These conflicting points of view boil down to two diametrically opposed beliefs: 1. We live in a friendly universe of abundance; or 2. We live in a hostile universe of scarcity.

King and Fromm added, *"According to Nielsen's 'Global Survey on Corporate Social Responsibility,' 43% of global consumers said they are willing to spend more for a product or service that supports a cause. And businesses are responding in kind. According to the 2012 IEG Sponsorship report, cause* *marketing programs in North America alone totaled $1.7 billion.*"[2]

Here's the real acid test in our culture: consumers will now spend more money for products and services that create benefits for their community. Plus, current statistics on volunteerism reveal that more and more people are giving generously to help others, without the crisis of a catastrophe.

This is evolution, an expansion of compassion—or some might say a return to traditional values. The transformation from "me" to "we" is trending. *This* is what consciousness is doing, expanding from separation into connection.

More and more individuals are consciously choosing this path. They are paying more for products and services that support good causes. This is developing a new class of leaders, many of them using their businesses to support wellbeing and even transformation in themselves and their employees and doing good for their communities and the world at large.

The "business of consciousness" is becoming a mainstream / sidestream marriage, progressing beyond human survival towards thriving in a future that is taking shape in unlikely ways. Our future needn't be as bleak as dystopian science fiction films and doomsday prophets portray. If we can't find convincing evidence in the news, perhaps we *can* find it in our own homes and neighborhoods. Global change always begins with local actions.

***What if we could create profit and wholeness
simultaneously in work and play?***

INSIGHT
*New business leaders are emerging,
supporting profit and wellbeing.
I am such a leader.*

ACTION
*Today, notice opportunities to lead at work.
Engage with one holistic opening.*

Celebrate your expanding leadership capacity.

Chapter Thirty-Nine, September 14   SUMMER

BECOMING FULLY OURSELVES

We may come to fully know ourselves through returning to nature and reclaiming our citizenry in the web of all life. Here is a timeless reality, known as a deep and enduring feeling of belonging in the world. Richard Jefferies writes about his contact with a tree: *"...to know from the actual touch of its rugged bark that the past is living now."*[1]

When was the last time you touched a tree? For some people, incredibly, the answer is never. That world "out there" remains out there, a barely observed necessity surrounding a life of industry and abstraction. "The world" has become a concept, not an organism. And it's certainly not where we feel that we truly belong. The wilderness? Dangerous and unproductive. Our modern response? As Joni Mitchell sang, *"They paved paradise and put up a parking lot."*[2]

Incredibly, some children never see the stars. They grow up in the city and there's too much light pollution. But many adults never bother to look. Why distract oneself from the demanding details of everyday life with something as irrelevant as the starry heavens! But there we are! The same life out there that lives in here.

There's a haunting line from Kabir, completing one of his amazing poems: *"... as the river gives itself into the ocean, what is inside me moves inside you."*[3] How tender, how compelling, how revealing of this great secret we are exploring, the rewards for surrendering our isolation, to connect with all that we are in the larger sense. "No man is an island," the saying goes, yet we have forgotten even the land beneath the waves that joins us. Imagine regaining the actual experience of that, of feeling deeply connected, of actually flowing through life. We are not separate from *all* others: all people and all species, including the invisible—those trillions of unseen life forms living within our own bodies and thriving all around us.

Imagine regaining that sense of belonging and the happiness that money can never buy. Being yourself, even as you read these words, brings a moment of relief from the hectic panic of civilized life. May this moment of exploration continue through the moments of this day. May you seize the day and—more than the day—seize the very essence of life as you expand your awareness to include all forms of life, with you in the midst, inexorably interwoven with it all.

What if you could regain the experience
of being connected,
of flowing together with everyone
and everything in your life?

INSIGHT
The universe is friendly.
I am welcomed and I belong in the web of all life.

ACTION
Today, deepen your connection with others
through full attention.
As you see them, welcome them as aspects of one source.
Notice how that feels.

Celebrate your ability to consciously increase
the experience of oneness.

SUMMER INTO FALL

Summer is the flowering, the flourishing that brings truth more fully into expression. You find yourself more naturally able to open to the experience of the truth of love, which is far beyond the subjective interior of your own being, beyond the mere recognition that the essence of yourself is part of the one loving energy of life. Now you are having the experience, and the objective reflections in your environment have changed. Be different, see different, experience different.

It is all the same; it is all the same love, the same blissful consciousness. Subject (you) and object (others and your environment) are the same. There is only one love and it is flowering in the season of summer. You are living love.

Because you are living love, your personal seeking is over. Your attention turns to contribution. How can you personally contribute to a better future? It is time now to give your gifts in the world.

Everyone has their gifts and everyone will contribute in their own way. For those who have tracked through the seasons of their awakening and become conscious of the process, they are in position to help midwife the same emergence in others. Ultimately, all of humankind is destined to evolve from the dominance of egocentric illusory separation to the truth of trans-egocentric unity.

You have been doing this, now you can show others the way. True leaders are those who know the way because they have walked it, because they continue to walk it. Your expanded ability to live love will show itself in various ways but one obvious one is the lessening of conflict in your life. All conflict is born of the illusory separation of object and subject. Because you have graduated into a heightened trans-egoic experience, conflict is reduced in your personal interactions. Now you can help that happen in the world around you.

All true and lasting conflict resolution comes because of a holistic experience of love. We can see the lack of this from the ongoing eruption of racism and violent bigotry ransacking the American heartland in the 21st century. The civil rights movement made significant gains and we can applaud the bravery of those who gave their lives to this. But it was incomplete. Obviously, because the separation and cruel judgment continues. Love renews all things.

You can lead the way to resolution of such conflict because you are open to the oneness and peace, the deep and lasting resolution of conflict that results from living love. Your demonstration of this will affect every one of your relationships and contribute to the radical shift in collective consciousness that is the only true way to reduce conflict and suffering.

Opening to this truth costs you nothing except the loss of loneliness. Awakening through the seasons of your enlightenment has been a choice you made, over and over again. Now, here in the turning of summer into fall, you are emerging as a leader, an ordinary person living an extraordinary life.

It is time to offer your gifts fully into the world.

PART FOUR

WELCOME TO FALL

WELCOME TO FALL

"The eternal wisdom made all things in love.
In love they all depend, to love they all return."[1]
Farid ud-Din Attar

"Love is space and time made perceptible to the heart."[2]
- Marcel Proust

Life is a circle of one, ever returning into itself, ever renewing, eternal. Life moves through four seasons with no end or beginning and all living beings on the earth ride that wave, gestating, growing, flowering into fullness, and then returning to source. Having this conscious experience indicates the achievement of a holistic awareness of the oneness of love. But this is not a linear experience progressing neatly from one stage to the other; everything of that circle blends together and exists in this eternal now.

Fall is the season of harvest, revelation of the seed in its fullness. Carrot seeds produce carrots, a fox embryo becomes a fox, a Chinese baby becomes a Chinese adult. The completion of autumn also produces new seeds for gestation through winter.

In fall, we celebrate both the harvest and the seeding, and we embrace the energy of completion that provides the energetic impetus for our new beginnings. Choice is often compelled by dissatisfaction and boredom, wanting something different from what we have. True choice arises from satisfaction with ongoing creativity.

Many people could honestly say, "I do not have what I want; I do not want what I have." From the fullness of holistic awareness we would say, "I am all I need." "I am" is the name of everything in creation, everything invested and sustained by life force. "I am" indicates natural, full integration in life, with nothing excluded. This is the complete experience of belonging: being as doing and doing as being, where true self-esteem has nothing to do with performance. We belong, fully valued, in the circle of one life.

"Love is space and time made perceptible to the heart." Now we begin to know what that means. It's harvest time and the abundance of life is peaking. And turning. We stand at a cross-roads, the pause between out-breath and in-breath, knowing love in this timeless moment of spacious freedom. Now we begin to know how to contribute to a better future, by continuing to participate in the evolution from egocentric to trans-egocentric experience. Now we know the secret: to live love.

We know that we will never find fulfillment outside of ourselves, because nothing exists outside of ourselves. We have expanded our awareness and know that nothing *can* exist beyond what we already are. Navigating our way through the travails of each day, we find peace and happiness in our choices, moment by moment, living love.

"Know that joy is rarer, more difficult,
and more beautiful than sadness.
Once you make this all-important discovery,
you must embrace joy as a moral obligation."[3]
-Andre Gide

Chapter Forty, September 21   FALL

RETURN TO THE HEART

Humanity gets an "A" for effort, for cleverly creating centuries of life experience without needing to consciously connect with spirit and nature. Of course, "effort" begins with "e," that lost grade between D and F, accurately grading our position on the razor's edge of the ultimate human failure, about to be handed an Eviction notice from our landlord. Climatologists call it "near-term extinction," and they're talking about the end of the human species during this century.

Does the urgency of today's environmental challenges suggest it might be time to change direction? They say, "If you don't change direction, you'll end up where you're headed." Funny, but true. How stubborn we've proven to be and we continue still.

Several years ago, during a TV spot with a Presidential candidate, the interviewer asked his governor about abstinence as a means of birth control, noting that it wasn't working in their state. The governor said that he believed in it. The interviewer repeated the statistics, that teen pregnancy had soared, despite their state-wide abstinence program. The governor repeated that he believed in it.

He wasn't willing to change direction, because of his belief, and that guaranteed ending up where they were going, with more and more teen pregnancies. I read later about a poll that concluded when individuals who hold irrational beliefs are confronted with the truth, they increase faith in their position!

Einstein advised that we won't solve our problems with the thinking we used to create them. What unlikely solutions might arise if we surrendered our stubborn loyalty to mental intransigence in favor of our hearts' natural responses to what is presented by *all* our senses? We might think (and feel... that's the point) differently. We might notice our neighbors and be known by them again. All of them, not just the human ones. We might become friends, again, all billions of species, and you know how we usually treat our friends and neighbors.

Returning to the heart, awakening the heart, we can enjoy Love for what it is, the intimacy natural to life in communion with itself. Rigid beliefs dam that flow, so giving in to Love is not weakness, it is courageous in a world that has valued stubbornness over adaptability. With gratitude, we can celebrate that breakthrough moment, demonstrated in the film *Bridge Over the River Kwai* when Alex Guinness's character came to his senses and said, *"What have I done?"*[1]

Each of us might also say that, suddenly awakening to how we've isolated ourselves from the joys of the heart through our own misplaced loyalties to belief over experience. But it's never too late to return to the heart; our family is waiting with open arms.

***What if I chose to release beliefs
when confronted with new facts?***

INSIGHT
*If we don't change direction,
we will end up where we are headed.
I am flexible and willing to change
what I believe.*

ACTION
*Think of something you are sure of. Google it.
Learn more; change your mind.
Notice how it feels to be proactive
about your personal growth.*

Celebrate your ability to choose something new.

FORGETTING YOURSELF

The growing crises on Spaceship Earth expose the insanity of our self-imposed quarantine. We humans have exceptionalized ourselves out of the web of life. But that doesn't change the fact of our lineage. Researcher Lynn Margulis wrote: *"Not only are bacteria our ancestors, but also… as the evolutionary anteced-ent of the nervous system, they invented consciousness."[1]*
Holy cow!
There's a lucky accident of spontaneous writing: cows *are* holy in India, and the phrase "sacred cow" has come to describe any belief that is held beyond questioning. What about our beliefs regarding life and consciousness? Can we actually stretch to entertain the possibility that what we just read might be true, that bacteria invented consciousness? It seems so utterly non-spiritual! As do bacteria themselves!
That's true enough, *if* our sacred cow is a concept of exclusion, that consciousness is selective. On that basis, how *could* one imagine bacteria playing a central role in anything but disease? Interestingly, it doesn't take much research to learn that bacteria *are* our ancestors and that they remain smarter than we are today, regardless of the marvels of our dysfunctional civilization. Yes, we've built skyscrapers and computers and our tomatoes last longer because we've injected them with rabbit genes, but microbial researchers report much greater complexity and intelligence hidden in a secret world where bacteria build their own cities, for instance, on the ocean floor, and heat them with electric cables of their own making! Who knew?
Germs have been the enemy for 150 years. But emerging research is disproving that bad guy theory. We need microbes. In fact, one doctor advised that we should think of them when we eat! We're feeding them too. The question is, which ones do we feed? Obviously, we want to support the helpful microbes and starve the thugs. Imagine, we have this invisible community of life within us. Again, who knew?

What's genuinely fascinating is the affection that the more open-hearted scientists come to feel for these invisible life forms. One of them wrote, *"As you look at these things, they become part of you. And you forget yourself. The main thing about it is you forget yourself."* [2]

This kind of forgetting is a good thing, to lose one's separate identity through an encounter with our neighbors. Ironically, that's exactly how it feels in moments of friendship, relaxing over a meal, laughing with each other. It's a brave but reachable extension to imagine that kind of loving camaraderie with all our neighbors.

We are not separate in fact, only in theory. The concept is powerful enough to convince us, hence our defensive stand towards nature. But She is not out to get us. We don't live in an unfriendly universe, only in unfriendly concepts. And those can change, obviously. Perhaps the simplest way to experience that change to inclusiveness is to simply acknowledge the community of life within us and take an empowering attitude towards them!

***What if your ancestors still live within your body,
as the microbes that invented consciousness?***

INSIGHT
*Bacteria invented consciousness.
I can return to the family of life and give up
my separate identity.*

ACTION
*Meditate on your beliefs
about consciousness and intelligence.
Today, release prejudice and exceptionalism
to embrace oneness.*

Celebrate your courage that challenges your beliefs.

Chapter Forty-Two, October 5   FALL

COME TO THE EDGE

French poet Guillaume Apollinaire wrote a compelling invitation for transcending fear with faith. This sort of heroism is what all of us need in the 21st century:

"Come to the edge," he said." We can't, we're afraid!" they responded. "Come to the edge," he said. "We can't, we will fall!" they responded. "Come to the edge," he said. And so they came. And he pushed them. And they flew."[1]

The value in his message is clear: to help us face our fears in life and move forward bravely. Yes, we will feel the fear but, as Shannon L. Alder wrote, *"Fear is the glue that keeps you stuck. Faith is the solvent that sets you free."*[2]

Faith like this is not meant to be reserved for special occasions; it's the opportunity of every moment and some moments are more challenging than others. *"Coming to the edge"* is not something we need to orchestrate... it happens automatically. In fact, many people feel like they *live* on the edge: the edge of bankruptcy, the edge of a health breakdown, the edge of divorce, etc. This calls to mind the legend of the Gordian knot. It has come to symbolize intractable problems too complicated for any simple solution. Yet, just as Alexander the Great purportedly cut the knot with a single swing of his sword, so can we cut through the complex challenges of our lives by coming to the edge and cutting ourselves free.

If that sounds risky, what's the alternative? Staying stuck, safe but suppressed, does not a fulfilling life make. Remember the poster: *"A ship in harbor is safe, but that is not what ships are built for."*[3] Playing safe is not what any of us are made for. But, in this culture, we are programmed to get our kicks from the risks others take—the athletes, celebrities and movie superheroes we admire from the sidelines.

Meanwhile, our souls yearn to be part of the action! What a difference, to leave the bench for the playing field, to be part of the team, to play our part, give our gifts! This is the empowerment that programs like this one aim for, to encourage you, whoever you are, to jump in the deep end of your life and learn to swim!

We have already flown. Remember that magical moment when, hurtling down the runway, our airplane suddenly lifted off, wheels separated from the runway, and we soared. Suddenly, we were flying! And, within seconds, our perspective changed radically. From above, everything looked fundamentally different. A strange beauty emerged, as tangled streets and litter turned into the symmetry of green and brown squares, lines of trees and curves of streets.

That's what happens when we come to the edge and take one more step. The question is not "if" you and I will do that, it's "when." Will we wait until the final leap all of us make at death or will we choose to experience that kind of leap consciously while we are alive? All we have to lose is our mediocrity!

What if you could fly?

INSIGHT
*Courage: coming the edge of the old
and flying into the new.
I am born to fly.*

ACTION
*Think of a complex problem you have.
Imagine a simple solution.*

***Celebrate your ability to bring resolution
through imagination.***

DEATH IS NOT THE END

Birth, life, death, rebirth .....

Life proceeds in an endless circle, not in a straight line. There are no straight lines in nature. Nature is cyclical, moving through seasons with no beginning and no end. Humans have disconnected from this pattern and the results are devastating, both to ourselves and to nature. We torture Mother Earth while we commit species suicide, contributing to the greatest rates of species extinctions this planet has ever experienced.[1] Our disconnection and ignorance may even produce the very thing we have feared – our own end, the near term extinction of humanity.

Ironically, the one way to prevent this unnatural death is to embrace the real one. Death is not the end but there *is* death. No flower blooms forever. Every human life comes to an end. Or, it seems to. Those who subscribe to theories of reincarnation believe we return, that we live many lives, learning lessons, burning off karma, and evolving towards enlightenment.

This conviction can breed complacency. "Oh well, if I don't do it in this life, I'll do it in the next one." Some hope this will be their last incarnation. "I'm going to complete my 'work' and go home."

That's real faith! How do we know… for sure? It's not like there's an army of reporters with true stories of death and rebirth. Is it really safe to bank on this belief, or does it make more sense to go for it in this life and then see what happens later?

My sense is that death is not the end, that there may never be a final incarnation. The fundamental idea of "completion" is probably flawed, because it arises from the experience of separation. "I am separate. I live as a human until I die. Then something mysterious happens and I return to do this again (as a human) or I remain… somewhere. Maybe in Heaven, maybe not!" For one thing, this perspective elevates humans and excludes other life forms, of which there are trillions. Would we really only return to repeat life as a human? How likely is that, given the uncountable options? And why would we return to earth? I'm not sure that's an appealing prospect for many of us!

Death is not the end. Yes, the bloom fades, the flower withers and dies, but it returns to the eco-system and continues without interruption, always connected. So too with our bodies, whether we bury or burn them. But we are more than our bodies. We are an in-dwelling spirit, an eternal spark of light in the star-filled universe. How could that light separate itself from *the* light for very long? In a body, in the soil, in the wind, in a dimension beyond imagination, we live as all life does, forever.

This can be a comforting theory or an empowering experience. How to evolve into that? The simplest way is to immerse ourselves in the system we are eternally part of (in theory) until we experience the reality. Nature beckons... no theories there, just the neighborhood where all of us belong.

What if you embraced your immortality?

INSIGHT
*The way to prevent the unnatural death of humanity
is to embrace the natural human one.
I am alive forever, living love.*

ACTION
*Dare to imagine your death.
Notice the feelings that arise.*

Celebrate the eternal nature of your true self.

Chapter Forty-Four, October 19   FALL

GIVE UP HOPE FOR A BETTER PAST

Love is not a sentiment, it's a force, *the* force that guides the stars and beats our hearts. Love has its own laws and to truly love one another means to obey those laws and hold ourselves and each other accountable.

"Love one another"[1] was the new commandment that Jesus left us with and we have utterly failed to understand what he meant and to do what he said. Loving someone does not mean being nice to them. Jesus was a warrior. Remember, he heaved the money changers out of the temple. He railed against the religious leaders of his day, scorning them as a "generation of vipers." This is far from the beliefs we hold about love and what it means to be truly loving.

To love one another demands, first, personal authenticity, to be true to love yourself. How do you do this? First, you must be honest. Look in the mirror and you will see many faces, all aspects of a complex being who lives in this world as a multitude of beings. You are all of these and you are one with them all. The one is the many; the many are one.

This is a popular spiritual mantra. What does it really mean? The one is the many—everything is part of the one. The many are one—every aspect of creation carries the essence of the one.

So, the first step in carrying out this new commandment is to begin loving all those parts of yourself and hold them all accountable to the laws of love. They say that your personality shows up when you don't. If you are not authentic, embracing all aspects of yourself in their wholeness, rather than identifying with just one of them (your personality of the moment), then you are not really present.

You are what you seek. This is true for all of us. The seeking for wholeness is seeking what I already am, what you already are. Experiencing this deeply requires that we stop identifying as consumers. We are creators and we create through the many aspects of our selves. Again, the many are one, the one is the many.

Deluded by a futile search for a different kind of enlighten-ment, we've judged ourselves, sometimes to the point of giving up. In any room full of people almost half of them have considered suicide. But every death temptation is part one of rebirth.

It all comes to rest in the moment. In order to be happy in this present moment, you must be willing to give up all hope for a better past or future. This is it! In order to fully enjoy the pre-sent, you must be willing to give up those addictive echoes from your wounded past and your dreams of future fulfillment. Love is happening now.

***What if you could accept your many selves
as aspects of the one you?***

INSIGHT
*The many are one, the one is the many.
I am what I am seeking.*

ACTION
*Make a list of the roles you play during any given week.
Practice playing them, not being them.*

Celebrate your many-faceted being.

LOVE IS WHAT YOU ARE

"While we cannot alter the nature of love,
we can choose to defy its dictates or thrive within its walls.
Those with the wisdom to do so will heed their hearts
and draw strength from their relatedness,
and they will raise their children to do likewise."[1]
- Thomas Lewis, Fari Amidi, Richard Lannon

Love is what we want. But love, true love, can never arrive to satisfy until we know that love is what/who we are. Imagine: all the millions of stories about love... How many of them even approach this understanding, let alone champion it or—even better—guide us into the experience? That's not the love story we read and watch. That one perpetuates separation, that love comes to us from elsewhere, from someone else.

Not so. Love is what we are. Love is what we share, lover to lover. How does it feel to conceive of love this way? "Love is what I am." If you can suspend self-judgment and just be with this declaration, repeating it silently, you open yourself to trans-formation.

Love is more than a feeling. Love beats our hearts. Love steers the stars. The experience of this is true love—even in these moments while you read these words—and it is intoxicating. Now, what if love could become an all-encompassing, every-day experience, not dependent upon others? What if there were a simple way to achieve this?

Love lives in nature, including and beyond whatever we can readily see or hear or smell or touch or taste or feel or even dream. Sit by a stream. Pause in a grove of scrub oaks. Lie in a field of grass. Day-dreaming, flirting with sleep, sinking into a world without people, it is easy to reconnect with the love that flows so freely in this natural world.

Now, imagine in your mind's eye that you are there in that nature sanctuary and notice (if you can) a shift from object orien-tation to awareness of relationship. Everything in nature is connected. How do you feel out there? *One with* **or** *separate from*? We've held our human selves separate but we can return. Our minds have built an artificial world, which we have come to prefer to the natural one, with predictably devastating results.

Think about how we've sourced our technology. You'd imagine we would have referenced the genius in systems that have functioned successfully for many millions of years. Uh, not so much. What we've created bears little resemblance to the way natural systems work. Ours and Hers are different in many fundamental ways but the primary difference is between synergy and separation, cooperation and competition. Our version is exhausting!

Return yourself into the embrace of Mother Nature and know that love is the same in every living form. Love is what you are.

***What if you could know that love is
the essential core nature of who you are?***

INSIGHT
*Love is more than a feeling. Love beats our hearts.
Love steers the stars. Love is what I am.*

ACTION
*Visit nature. Sit silent and still. Perceive your connection with all
your relations. Journal about how this feels.*

***Celebrate your belonging within the
whole community of life.***

THE HARVEST

Harvest is both a time of reaping and sowing. Plants offer up their bounty for consumption and seeding. The end is also the beginning and the cycle of life continues. By contrast, human culture is linear. Growth is constant and necessary to sustain civilization, which means that civilization—the way we have built it—is ultimately unsustainable. In the natural cycles of life, growth must be complemented with rest. Farmers know this; soil needs "down time".

The seasons give us a daily reminder of this cycle. It's fascinating how successful we have been in ignoring them! We also ignore the sun, which powers the planet, choosing oil for our fuel instead. Not to mention developing nuclear power, even more toxic. We regard pagan worship of the sun as foolish, favoring a theoretical God instead, a God with rules, different for different faiths, carefully defined in books and sermons. Meanwhile, the truth of nature abounds with natural laws that produce harmony and abundance.

This is ignored by most of us but not by everyone. For instance, the Biomimicry Institute explores how to copy nature. They define biomimicry as *"an approach to innovation that seeks sustainable solutions to human challenges by emulating nature's time-tested patterns and strategies. The goal is to create products, processes, and policies—new ways of living—that are well-adapted to life on earth over the long haul."[1]*

These new ways of living acknowledge cycles. Harvest time gives us not only abundance of completion, it provides the seeds for the next cycle of growth. Typically, in human activities, we ignore these starting points in favor of making up what's to come next on our own, solely from our imaginations. This destroys coherence and substitutes human cleverness for the flow of expanding life. We lose the order and synergistic relationships that abound in nature and juggle disparate aspects of a chaotic creation, each part in conflict with the other (for instance, environmentalism in conflict with business).

We can choose to reverse course at any moment by embracing the dual nature of harvest time, honoring both the completion and the beginning, simultaneously available for experience in the eternal now.

We are never starting from scratch. Seeds for the future are always present at the moment of completion. Of course we never learned about this (or most of the other truly important aspects of being a human being!) and so we grow up ignorant of how to grow our futures instead of trying to make them up as best we can, independent of the intelligence of Gaia.

There are cycles in our lives. Just as most farmers understand when to plant, according to the phase of the moon, so we can learn to create according to the rhythms that are guiding all living beings. There is a right (and wrong) time for everything.

What if you awakened to the cycles in your life and began harvesting the potential of each moment?

INSIGHT
*Humans have ignored the natural world
to create an artificial substitute.
I belong in the natural world.*

ACTION
*Consider your relationship with the sun.
Journal: I love the sun because...*

Celebrate your relationship with the sun.

CELEBRATION

Celebration is typically reserved for winning, although occasion-
ally an athlete celebrates his competitor's brilliant shot. On the
rare times that happens, the audience inevitably cheers. We sense
the rightness of it, selfishness giving way to the generosity of
mutual enjoyment.

In the autumn months, we can discover opportunities to
reflect with appreciation on the full harvest of the year, not just
parts of it. As the sun moves, the weather changes, and our
bodies begin to prepare and adapt to the next season. We shift
from production to gathering and storing. It's the time for celebration and reflection.

As the year comes full circle, reflect on your personal commitment to ongoing growth and celebrate the expansion of your
awareness this has brought you. This week, honor your conscious
choice to continue awakening to your wholeness. Acknowledge
yourself for allowing the awakening impulse to work in your life,
for accelerating it with your choices. It is available for all of us
but not all of us welcome it.

What if this were your personal priority? Why wouldn't it
be? The baubles of civilization are no kind of substitute. There's
nothing wrong with using what's available and enjoying it all, but
that's different from worshipping the jewels of the material
world.

This is the season of the year for celebrating the greatest of
gifts: love. Nothing in the material world can match the value of
love, the opportunity to enlighten, to illuminate the grandeur of
ourselves, to live love. It's beyond even imagination, what we
already sense, a deepening experience of living love as who we
are and sharing that with each other. That defines the truth of
"being in love."

Appropriate festivities this week can include special meditation times of celebration. Buckminster Fuller defined wealth as
"the number of days forward you can live."[1] As you prepare for
Thanksgiving festivities, step back from the food and parties to

consider this definition of wealth: the number of days you have before you. Life is a gift, every day, every moment, and not to be wasted in unconscious busyness but relished in the embrace of love.

Thanksgiving in our country is often a celebration of excess. Perhaps this year you can change that. Food and drink... wonderful. But what's the real point? What's the real celebration? Material comfort, or the blessing of awareness? Awareness of what? The opportunity that living here in the 21st century has brought to us all: to awaken to our role in the greatest drama that has ever unfolded in human experience. Imagine: to be alive at this time on the planet! What a challenge, what an opportunity, what a privilege!

It only takes a moment to focus appreciation for what you are blessed to experience in your life. You and I represent a graced minority on the planet; we have the space and time to read! Celebrate the true gifts of the season.

What if you could celebrate and
reflect with appreciation every day?

INSIGHT
Autumn is the season for reflection and celebration.
I am wealthy in the days yet to live.

ACTION
Reflect on and celebrate the year
that is nearing completion.
Write two lists: the good and bad for the year.
Contemplate the lessons learned.

Celebrate your ability to love it all.

THE VALUE OF APPRECIATION

The value of appreciation is implicit in its true meaning. When we appreciate someone or something, we increase value. Just as an object depreciates—like a car or a printer—losing value over time, relationships can gain or lose value, depending on our choices to appreciate or depreciate.

Appreciation can be proactive. Usually it's reactive, that is, we express appreciation in response to something. "Thanks for that, I appreciate it." But we can also initiate appreciation, for no reason other than we choose to. Choosing to appreciate, choosing to increase value, is one very simple and deliberate way to grow love in your daily experience.

Seen this way, it makes no sense to withhold appreciation. What couldn't benefit from having its value increased? Obviously, there are things we don't appreciate, like a sore back. Really? Perhaps there's another way to look at even this. Why is the back sore? Might not there be a message here: "Rest. See a chiropractor. Exercise."

What's not to appreciate about a message like that? So, even in this case, there's something to appreciate. "Thanks for the heads up!" How many messages like that do we routinely miss, because we're too busy making a living!? Slowing down to "smell the roses" is simultaneously an opportunity to slow down and experience the rest of what we've been missing in the express lane.

This week, explore expressing appreciation proactively and see what happens. For instance, you might thank a gas station attendant: "I wanted to tell someone here that I appreciate the service I always get, thank you." Experimenting with this, one comes to a vastly different experience of "others." This person that was invisible to you before, just the guy pumping gas, shows up as a unique human… one of a kind, suddenly present in your life and interacting in a way that beckons your appropriate investment. A simple thank you—what that can do!

Simple as this is, appreciation seeds magic. When any of us feel appreciated, especially when someone volunteers it spontaneously, we get a message about ourselves: "I have value. I am appreciated." We can never know what impact that might have in a stranger's life. I've heard stories about people on the brink of suicide who turned back to life, because of a simple extension of caring from a stranger, someone they never met again and who would never know they saved a life.

Love does not flow *only* in response; love is proactive and appreciation is a wonderful way to express it. Whoever said giving is better than receiving only had it half right. Giving and receiving are equally valuable and enjoyable. Remember, we experience what we express. So, when we are appreciative, we experience that flowing through us, before it gets to our "target." Appreciation, love, forgiveness... who wouldn't want to experience more of these? Here's the simple answer: give it! And, simultaneously, receive it.

What if you chose to appreciate for no reason
other than to express love?

INSIGHT
Appreciation increases value.
I am love in expression
through appreciation.

ACTION
Appreciate others spontaneously,
not for what they do but for who they are.
Notice how others react when you appreciate them this way.

Celebrate your ability to increase love through appreciation.

FORGIVENESS IS MEDICINE

Forgiveness is medicine. Like any medicine, it works best when the dose is correct and it is applied in an accurate way. Even some poisons can become miracle healers when administered wisely. Likewise with forgiveness.

When forgiveness is premature, when someone tries to forgive before it is genuine, it masks the truth. A person may smile and say, "I forgive you." Meanwhile, underneath, they continue to seethe with resentment. Forgiveness becomes a poison for them. You can't fake the truth.

The same toxic result occurs when a person refuses the medicine. "I can't accept her forgiveness." What is he really saying? "I am judging her and I will never stop judging her. I will hold onto this grudge no matter what." This kind of rigidity is not the way life works. Such a stubborn attitude establishes an obstruction that will increase imbalance and disharmony—in the one who refuses to participate in forgiveness (for whatever reason).

On the other hand, when someone accepts forgiveness and fully feels what they feel, when they are honest and wholehearted with that acceptance, they can find themselves suddenly liberated from the emotions that burdened them. This is a healing alchemy and it happens in the heart.

In my recent book, *Forgiving the Unforgivable*, I wrote: *"Like the mind-field, the heart-field also has two polarities, positive and negative, which we represent as the two primary emotions of love and fear. The default dominant for the heart-field is also negative which means that, for most people, fear is usually dominant. So, to balance this level, we emphasize the non-dominant polarity – love. We shift our emotional emphasis from fear to love."*[1]

The application of forgiveness as a medicine is one proactive way to shift from fear to love. There are three steps: 1. Fully feel what you are feeling. 2. Acknowledge that this is primarily about you, not another person or the situation. 3. Know that this is part of your own healing journey.

Some say they can forgive but never forget. That's true, but what is it that we will never forget? The injustice, the pain, our judgment? Or, do we choose to remember what we learned from the experience? True forgiveness heals. If the wound still festers, if the pain remains acute, forgiveness hasn't happened yet, not fully. The deep ache of loss will never pass, for instance, if one suffered the tragic loss of a family member in a violent crime. But forgiveness works its healing wonders even here. Stories abound of reconciliation between victims and perpetrators, heart-felt enough to provoke deep healing for all.

So, forgive. It can help to voice it, even silently: "I forgive you, as I forgive myself." Or "Thank you, I accept your for-giveness." Each step involves truth-telling and the development of emotional "muscles." Here is a simple process for increasing love in your personal experience, one that requires no one else but you and your own choice.

***What if you could easily forgive and accept forgiveness,
without holding on to the past?***

INSIGHT
*Forgiveness is a powerful medicine,
in the right dose and at the right time.
I am a doctor of forgiveness.*

ACTION
*Consider those you have not forgiven and those
from whom you have not accepted forgiveness.
Follow the three-step process for each
until you are clear of judgment.*

***Celebrate your ability to give and receive
healing through forgiveness.***

BEING GUIDED

All of us need help. Beyond what we naturally receive from parents and teachers, the "mentoring" role is often played by other relatives: a kindly grandmother, special friends, employers, ministers or other spiritual leaders and, increasingly, coaches.

Coaching was once primarily reserved for athletes. In fact, the word "coach" referred to a team coach. But in the 21st century, coaching is also available to individuals, not just athletes but for anyone perfecting the skills of living. Coaching is now used to support achieving business success, managing health challenges and saving relationships. And the paradigm has shifted from just "winning" to succeeding, whatever that might look like over the long term.

In *Co-active Coaching*, authors House, House, Sandahl, and Whitworth write, *"A coach is someone who will absolutely tell the truth – the truth about where clients are strong, for example, and where they hold back and give up, deny, or rationalize."*[1]

This kind of honest guidance can be a lifesaver. For instance, let's imagine a client has a drinking problem. Their coach might succeed in impressing upon them how significant the danger is, to the point where they "remember" not to have another beer before driving home from a party. Let's say it works. So, come party night, why do they say no, denying their addiction and the immediate pleasure it gives them? It happens because the wisdom of their coach was still with them, present somewhere in their awareness like a guardian angel whispering in their ear. And that whisper might save a life.

We don't need to deliberately hold back and give up, deny, or rationalize. It's not about sacrifice like that. Addictions are unconscious habits that cause us to react automatically when we are triggered. If we knew we were doing that and had an alternative, we might stop. Here's where a guide – by whatever name – comes in. She might see the habitual pattern when we don't. If she is skilled, she can then help *us* see it. Once seen, we have a choice: change or not. And change is not just about stopping something, it's about replacing it. One of the simplest examples is diet. There are so many alternatives to junk food these days... and they taste better!

Of course, just because we become aware of an old habit and decide we want to exchange it for a new one doesn't mean that we're going to do it. If only change were that easy! How many people continue smoking, for instance, long after they "know" it's harmful to their health. No, awareness is not enough, there needs to also be motivation. The usual motivations – fear or pleasure – don't always work. In fact, they tend to peter out. How long do New Year's Resolutions usually last?

Visionary motivation begins with a clear articulation of the rewards ahead, *if* we make the change. It helps to receive assistance from a coach but, ultimately, the ongoing guidance comes from the vision itself. And we can create our visions of reward for ourselves, to continue motivating our ongoing change.

What if you could create a tangible vision
of the rewards associated with
making a difficult change?
Wouldn't that motivate you to stick with it?

INSIGHT
A coach can help people change.
I am ultimately responsible
for my own guidance.

ACTION
Consider stuck areas in your life.
Contemplate who might coach you.
Reach out for help.

Celebrate your courage;
asking for help is a sign of strength.

Chapter Fifty-One, December 7   FALL

SHINE LIGHT ON THE PATH

If you're hiking in the dark with a friend and he has a flashlight, you appreciate him shining it on the path, not in your eyes. Likewise, if someone has wisdom to share, it's helpful when they relate it to your life. Being assaulted by uninvited "advice" from a person who's convinced they can help you is actually abusive.

This brings to mind the story of a Boy Scout who returned to headquarters with bruises and torn clothes. "What happened to you?" his Scout Master asked. "I helped an old lady across the street," he replied. "Well, why are you all beat up then?" The scout confessed, "She didn't want to go!"

This is the unconscious missionary habit, helping others because *we* think they need it. Who made us so wise and infallible? What about consulting them, what about getting permission first?

Shine light on the path. This is how we help each other. And, taking it another step, *be* light on the path. Support another's journey as an equal, rather than being superior, even if you think you've traveled more miles. How would you know?

We might be surprised. The person we assume needs our wisdom might be smarter than we think. Here's a different way to look at this: wisdom is always an exchange; we receive from each other. If we assume that, then we become alert to discover what we can learn from those we may be helping. How vital an attitude shift this is for all teachers! Teachers, we have much to learn from our students.

Walt Whitman wrote, *"You shall no longer take things at second or third hand, or look through the eyes of the dead, nor feed on the spectres in books, you shall not look through my eyes either, nor take things from me, you shall listen to all sides and filter them from your self."*[1]

This self-filtering is not a skill we learned in school. In fact, we've all learned the opposite, to look to leaders, to rely on rules, to stay between the lines and behave. Ironically, look who we pick for our heroes? Rule breakers! Rebels! Those who are uniquely themselves, not rule followers!

Our true path takes us from culture clone to authentic individual. Yes, others can help us, but only when they help illuminate our path. It's wonderful to walk together, to share a path, but ultimately, we each have our own unique, personal path. True friendship is respecting that and helping each other stay true to that, no matter what.

This week, notice any tendencies to jump in with free advice and, instead, pause and step back for a moment of respect. Ask yourself, "would this help my friend or am I just revealing my superiority?" And then remind yourself that the best support we can offer another is to shine our own authentic light by being fully present with no agenda.

What if you could hold your tongue
and avoid giving advice;
instead, be fully present with others,
listening and appreciating?

INSIGHT
The best advice is to be fully present.
I am most helpful when I am present.

ACTION
Notice your relationships and when
you are inclined to offer advice.
Wait a moment, keep listening,
and see what happens.

Celebrate your wisdom as patience.

COMPLETION

This is the final calendar entry, completing the journey of the year on the Winter Solstice. But, like the seasons themselves, this book is a circle, it too continues week after week without end.

The year is a cycle, moving through four seasons, as we are representing in these weekly writings. We are approaching completion now, of the book and of the year, but that's arbitrary. We chose to begin with winter... we could have just as easily begun with spring, or summer, or fall. The beginning is where we are, which is also an ending. This is the true nature of life as a circle.

Every moment is a beginning and an ending, the "alpha and omega," all contained in the present moment. The harvest includes both the fruit and the seeds and fulfillment does not arise from ignoring one for the other. This is exactly what we tend to do in our myopic culture: we grab for short-term gratification (fruit) and neglect the long-term value (seeds). This creates a barren future.

Nature does not struggle to make up what comes in spring! In fact, spring is a symbol for hope. We have faith that spring *will* come, no matter how bleak winter might seem. Likewise, the sun rises! There is never a morning when it doesn't.

In *The Clock of the Long Now*, Stewart Brand wrote, *"Civilization is revving itself into a pathologically short attention span. ... Some sort of balancing corrective to the short-sightedness is needed—some mechanism or myth that encourages the long view and the taking of long-term responsibility, where "the long term" is measured at least in centuries."* [1]

To measure the long term in centuries requires a fundamental shift in personal identity. At this winter-solstice moment, when it is customary to celebrate the arrival of the divine child, let us declare that birth within ourselves.

"I am the seed and the harvest of a divine child. I am much more than a single human, defined within my individual life span. I am spread broad across the centuries. My ancestors live within me still, as genes and DNA. The ideas I have shared, whatever I have built, will continue to grow through my children and my friendships.

"I was never only this reflection in the mirror. I am privileged to live in a time when expanding awareness is flowing through human consciousness at an accelerating rate. We are waking up together! The sun is rising after a long night of ignorant disconnection from each other, from ourselves, and from the universal web of life which is Love."

"I am living love."

These words may seem grandiose, a pronouncement of some kind. But they are just words, words that hopefully convey the magnificence of life. But, as we all know, the vast majority of life is made up of simple moments, not grand in any particular way at all. The authentic measure is "realness." How real is it for us, how real is our experience of living love? Regardless, as with everything, practice makes perfect!

What if you could experience completion
and beginning in the same moment?

INSIGHT
Life moves through seasons.
I am a divine child, ever birthing myself anew.

ACTION
Contemplate this turning moment
between seasons and years.
Pick four highlights of the year
and four lessons learned.

Celebrate your true nature – living love.

FALL INTO WINTER

Mission accomplished.

Another year is completing. The seasons continue without end, beyond this end, which is also another beginning. In this solstice moment, as we celebrate the birth of the divine child, we also celebrate the potential of love that is seeded to harvest in each moment.

Winter is coming. The time nears to let go of your busyness and relax into the slow comfort of this new season. Light gives way to dark and the opportunity for seeds to gestate in secret. What seeds live within you, ready for this time of nurturing?

Now our focus naturally changes from outward to inward. All that we have loved this year is fading in our awareness as the dominance of our experience shifts from accomplishment to contemplation, from activity to rest.

No season is better than any other; all have their place in the ongoing tapestry of life woven together with the cords of love. You have been living love all year and focusing your consciousness week after week with the specific guidance in this book.

Now, in celebration, it all blends into one single message:

You are the love you have been seeking.

"You are a volume in the divine book
A mirror to the power that created the universe
Whatever you want, ask it of yourself
Whatever you're looking for can only be found
Inside of you."[1]
- Rumi

CONCLUSION

Thank you for undertaking this reading adventure. You may be at the physical end of this book, but the year marches on and the chapters are designed so you can recycle back through the year when you return to where you began.

When you complete the 52 lessons, regardless of where you started, we recommend that you read through it a second time and review your journal notes for the same date as you re-read. This will give you a way to measure how much you have grown during the past 12 months and how your awakened living has evolved. Remember to continue journaling so you can repeat again, if you wish.

While high-profile leaders like the Dalia Lama are of immense benefit for the awakening of humanity, they celebrate individuals like you and me for being our authentic selves and finding ways to give our own gifts. This heralds the age of the "local hero," where real, positive change arises one person at a time in a grass-roots movement of expanding awareness.

Living an Awakened Life: The Lessons of Love has immediate and long-term benefits, as you have been experiencing. Thank you for choosing this path. May love guide your way.

ᐤ

ENDNOTES

WINTER
Welcome to Winter

1. Edith Sitwell, as quoted by Georgia Varozza, 501 Time-Saving Tips Every Woman Should Know, Harvest House Publishers, Feb. 1, 2015, pg. 46.

2. Attributed to Francis of Assisi ("St. Francis"), as quoted in goodreads.com, https://www.goodreads.com/quotes/876987-what-you-are-looking-for-is-what-is-looking

December 21

1. Jean Liedloff, Chapter Six, "Society," The Continuum Concept: In Search Of Happiness Lost, January 22, 1986, page 150.

2. Laura Sewall, "The Skill of Ecological Perception," Ecopsychology, Restoring the Earth, Healing the Mind, Counterpoint, Sierra Book Club series, January 1, 1995, page 204.

3. A Native American Prayer for Peace, "World Healing Prayers," U.N. Day of Prayer for World Peace, WorldhealingPrayers.com, http://www.worldhealingprayers.com/2.html

4. David Abram, "Merleau-Ponty and the Voice of the Earth," wildethics.org, originally published in Environmental Ethics, volume 10 (1988), pp. 101-120, http://www.wildethics.org/essay/merleau-ponty-and-the-voice-of-the-earth/

December 28

1. William Carlos Williams, "Book II," Asphodel, That Greeny Flower, New Directions Publishing, November 1, 1994, page 19.

2. Erazim Kohak as quoted by Gregory Ripley in "Chapter Five, Nature Meditations," Tao of Sustainability: Cultivate Yourself to Heal the Earth, Three Pine Press, December 12, 2015.

3. Carl Anthony, "Ecopsychology and the Deconstruction of White-ness," Ecopsychology, Restoring the Earth, Healing the Mind, published by Counterpoint, Sierra Book Club series, January 1, 1995, page 265.

January 4

1. Charles Eisenstein, The More Beautiful World Our Hearts Know Is Possible (Sacred Activism), North Atlantic Books, Third Edition, November 5, 2013, page 75.

2. Kathleen Miles, "Ray Kurzweil: In The 2030s, Nanobots In Our Brains Will Make Us 'Godlike,'" The World Post of The Huffington Post, October 1, 2015, http://www.huffingtonpost.com/entry/ray-kurzweil-nanobots-brain-godlike_560555a0e4b0af3706dbe1e2

January 11

1. David Banner, Kenneth J.M. MacLean, "The Law of Cause and Effect," Chapter 9, Frameshifting: A Path to Wholeness (Spiritual Dimensions), Loving Healing Press, March 24, 2008, page 138.

2. Beach Boys, Good Vibrations, single recording, Capitol Records, October 10, 1966.

3. The Giver, Dir. Phillip Noyce, Perf. Jeff Bridges, Brenton Thwaites, Odeya Rush, Meryl Streep, Katie Holmes, et.al., The Weinstein Company, 2014. Film.

4. Rhonda Zurn, "New study shows that yoga and meditation may help train the brain," Discover Science + Technology, University of Minnesota, September 25, 2014, http://discover.umn.edu/news/science-technology/new-study-shows-yoga-and-meditation-may-help-train-brain

5. Kaitlin Cassady et al, "The impact of mind-body awareness training on the early learning of a brain-computer interface", Technology Volume 02, Issue 03, 254, WorldScientific.com, September 2014, http://www.worldscientific.com/doi/abs/10.1142/S233954781450023X?%20query%20%20ID=%24%7BresultBean.queryID%7D&

January 18

1. Attributed to Socrates, as quoted in "Socrates>Quotes>Quotable Quote" in goodreads.com, https://www.goodreads.com/quotes/109203-beware-the-barrenness-of-a-busy-life

January 25

1. Attributed to the Buddha, as quoted by Deepak Chopra, "Walking the pathless path," Life section, The Times of India, February 4, 2011, http://timesofindia.indiatimes.com/life-style/Walking-the-pathless-path/articleshow/6299253.cms

February 1

1. Thomas Berry, as quoted by Sarah McFarland Taylor, Chapter 8, "Stations of the Earth," Green Sisters, Harvard University Press, September 1, 2009, page 256.

February 8

1. Attributed to Alain Aspect, "Alain Aspect," brainyquote.com, http://www.brainyquote.com/quotes/authors/a/alain_aspect.html

2. Anonymous, as quoted by Darren Poke, Better Life Coaching Blog, https://betterlifecoachingblog.com/2010/05/21/shoe-salesmen-in-africa-a-story-about-optimism/

February 15

1. John von Neumann, as quoted in wikipedia.org, "Technological singularity," paragraph 2, https://en.wikipedia.org/wiki/Technological_singularity.

2. Ray Kurzweil, The Singularity is Near, The Viking Press, 1st edition, September 22, 2005, page 7.

3. Richard Buckminster Fuller, Chapter 3, "Comprehensively Commanded Automation," Operating Manual for Spaceship Earth, Lars Muller, 1st edition, July 15, 2008, page 53.

February 22

1. Michael Brenner, "Thanks Social Media – Our Average Attention Span Is Now Shorter Than Goldfish," D!gitalist, SAP Magazine, 30-May-2014, paragraph 8, http://www.digitalistmag.com/lob/sales-marketing/2014/05/30/thanks-social-media-average-attention-span-now-shorter-goldfish-01251966

2. Ibid.

March 1

1. Psalm 127:1, King James Version of The Bible, biblegateway.com, https://www.biblegateway.com/verse/en/Psalm%20127%3A1

2. United Nations Commission on Human Rights as quoted by Gustavo Capdevila, "Human Rights: More Than 100 Million Homeless Worldwide," IPS (Inter Press Service), http://www.ipsnews.net/2005/03/human-rights-more-than-100-million-homeless-worldwide/

March 8

1. Thich Nhat Hanh, Chapter One, "We Are the Earth," Parallax Press, Love Letter to the Earth, June 17, 2013, page 8.

March 15

1. Queen Rania al Abdullah of Jordan, "The Blog: What Good is Technological Progress Without Moral Progress?" The Huffington Post, May 6, 2016, last paragraph, http://www.huffingtonpost.com/rania-al-abdullah/what-good-is-technological-progress-without-moral-progress_b_7217068.html

SPRING
Welcome to Spring

1. Thich Nhat Hanh, Your True Home: The Everyday Wisdom of Thich Nhat Hanh, Shambhala, November 1, 2011, page 209.

March 22

1. Zen proverb as quoted in "The Blog: Meditation, Demystified," The Huffington Post, March 17, 2013, http://www.huffingtonpost.com/dawn-gluskin/meditation_b_2382626.html

2. Attributed to Albert Einstein in various forms since first appearing as a similar quote in The New York Times, March 1929, "Relativity: A Hot Stove and A Pretty Girl," Quote Investigator, quoteinvestigator.com, http://quoteinvestigator.com/2014/11/24/hot-stove/

March 29

1. Rudolf Steiner, Chapter 1, How to Know Higher Worlds, A Modern Path of Initiation, Anthroposophic Press, 1994, page 36.

2. Rebecca Gladding, M.D., "This Is Your Brain on Meditation," Psychology Today, psychologytoday.com, May 22, 2013, https://www.psychologytoday.com/blog/use-your-mind-change-your-brain/201305/is-your-brain-meditation

3. Malcolm Gladwell, Outliers: The Story of Success, Little, Brown and Company, 1st edition, 2008.

April 5

1. Attributed to Socrates, Rachel McCarthy, An Empathetic World, https://anempatheticworld.com/2014/05/06/i-know-i-am-intelligent-because-i-know-that-i-know-nothing-socrates-2/

2. Attributed to Socrates, The Free Dictionary, thefreedictionary.com, http://www.thefreedictionary.com/Socratic+method

3. Matthew 7:7, King James Version of The Bible, biblehub.com, http://biblehub.com/matthew/7-7.htm

4. Attributed to Blaise Pascal, goodreads.com, https://www.goodreads.com/quotes/747889-small-minds-are-concerned-with-the-extraordinary-great-minds-with

April 12

1. Anonymous, sometimes attributed to Saint Bernard of Clairvaux and Virgil's "Aeneid." "The road to hell is paved with good intentions," wikipedia.org, https://en.wikipedia.org/wiki/The_road_to_hell_is_paved_with_good_i ntentions

April 19

1. Elizabeth Lesser, "Chapter 4: Toward a Spirituality of Wholeness," The Seeker's Guide (Previously published as The New American Spirituality), Villard, October 3, 2000, page 81.

April 26

1. Thomas Edison, as quoted by Christine Finn, "The People: Better to Fail Hopefully," Artifacts: An Archaeologist's Year in Silicon Valley, The M.I.T. Press, First Edition, November 1, 2001, page 90.

2. Jon Perry and Ted Kupper, "The Race Between Intelligence Augmentation and Artificial Intelligence (IA vs AI)," The Decline of Scarcity, http://declineofscarcity.com/?p=2312

May 3

1. Aldous Huxley, as quoted in "Aldous Huxley Interview," Huxley.net, http://www.huxley.net/ah/aldous_huxley.html

2. Doug Aamoth, "An Interview With Ray Kurzweil," *Time.com*, April 2, 2010, http://techland.time.com/2010/04/02/an-interview-with-ray-kurzweil/

3. The Borg, quoted in tagline, Star Trek: First Contact, Dir. Jonathan Frakes, Perf. Patrick Stewart, Jonathan Frakes, Brent Spiner, LeVar Burton, et.al., Paramount Pictures, 1996. Film.

4. Albert Einstein as quoted in an 1929 interview in "The Saturday Evening Post," Quote Investigator, quoteinvestigator.com, http://quoteinvestigator.com/2013/01/01/einstein-imagination/

May 10

1. Samuel Taylor Coleridge as quoted by Radin Dean, "Theme: Chapter 4, Meta-Analysis," The Conscious Universe: The Scientific Truth, HarperOne, Reprint edition June 30, 2009, page 55.

2. Max Muller, as quoted in "Friedrich Max Muller>Quotes>Quotable Quote," goodreads.com, https://www.goodreads.com/quotes/496874-a-flower-cannot-blossom-without-sunshine-and-man-cannot-live

3. Kate Yandell, "Revealing Metamorphosis," The Scientist, May 14, 2013, http://www.the-scientist.com/?articles.view/articleNo/35556/title/Revealing-Metamorphosis/

4. Darrick Dean, Is The Truth Out There? Lulu.com, 2nd edition, July 12, 2008, page 91.

May 17

1. Walt Whitman, as quoted in "Walt Whitman Quotes," BrainyQuote, brainyquote.com, http://www.brainyquote.com/quotes/quotes/w/waltwhitma383391.html

2. William Blake, as quoted by Arthur Quiller-Couch, ed., "489. The Tiger, The Oxford Book of English Verse: 1250-1900," Bartleby.com, http://www.bartleby.com/101/489.html

May 24

1. James Hillman, "The Thought of the Heart, II. The Heart of Beauty: Kalon Kagathon and Jung," The Thought of the Heart, and, The Soul of the World, Spring Publications, May 20, 1998, page 55.

2. Gottfried Benn, as quoted by Albert Hoffman, LSD, My Problem Child, MAPS.org, 4th edition, March 1, 2009, page 29.

3. Attributed to Socrates by Plato in "Apology 38A," as quoted in philosophypages.com, http://www.philosophypages.com/hy/2d.htm

4. Albert Hoffman, LSD, My Problem Child, MAPS.org, 4th edition, March 1, 2009, page 29.

June 1

1. John Taylor Gatto, Dumbing Us Down: The Hidden Curriculum of Compulsory Schooling, New Society Publishers, 2nd edition, February 1, 2002, page 60.

2. Attributed to Einstein, Icarus-falling.blogspot.com, http://icarus-falling.blogspot.com/2009/06/einstein-enigma.html

3. Attributed to Georg Wilhelm Friedrich Hegel, goodreads.com, https://www.goodreads.com/author/quotes/6188.Georg_Wilhelm_Friedrich_Hegel

4. John Taylor Gatto, Dumbing Us Down: The Hidden Curriculum of Compulsory Schooling, New Society Publishers, 2nd edition, February 1, 2002.

5. Richard Jeffries, "III.—A Ring-Fence: Conclusion," The Hills and the Vale, Read Books Ltd., 2015.

June 8

1. Stephen Harrod Buhner, Plant Intelligence and the Imaginal Realm: Beyond the Doors of Perception into the Dreaming of Earth, Bear & Company, 1st edition, May 3, 2014, page 19.

2. Ibid, page 19.

3. Ibid, page 19.

4. Aldo Leopold, A Sand County Almanac, Ballantine Books, Reprint edition, December 12, 1986, page 158.

June 15

1. Roy Orbison, "Only the Lonely," Lonely and Blue, Monument 45-421 label, May, 1960.

2. John Taylor Gatto, Dumbing Us Down: The Hidden Curriculum of Compulsory Schooling, New Society Publishers, 2nd edition, February 1, 2002, page 53.

3. Stephen Harding, as quoted in Stephen Harrod Buhner's Plant Intelligence and the Imaginal Realm: Beyond the Doors of Perception into the Dreaming of Earth, Bear & Company, 1st edition, May 3, 2014, page 328.

SUMMER
Welcome to Summer

1. Medieval song by unknown author in Middle English in 13th century England, "Sumer Is Icumen In," also referred to as "Cuckoo Song," wikipedia.org, https://en.wikipedia.org/wiki/Sumer_Is_Icumen_In

June 22

1. Attributed to Mark Twain, brainyquote.com, http://www.brainyquote.com/quotes/quotes/m/marktwain109624.html

2. Joe Friday, television character played by Jack Webb, "Dragnet," 1951-1959, as quoted in wikipedia.org, https://en.wikipedia.org/wiki/Dragnet_(franchise)

3. Richard "Rick" Blaine, film character played by Humphrey Bogart, "Casablanca," Dir. Michael Curtiz, Warner Bros., 1942, as quoted in infoplease.com, http://www.infoplease.com/askeds/editing-film-history.html

4. John Newton, "Amazing Grace," Olney Hymns, Buckinghamshire, England, 1779, as quoted in wikipedia.org, https://en.wikipedia.org/wiki/Amazing_Grace

5. Laura Sewall, "The Skill of Ecological Perception," from Eco-Psychology, 1st edition, a Sierra Club Books Publication, published by Counterpoint, 1995, page 203.

June 29

1. Reihan Salam, "A New Hippie Movement Has Some Families Returning to Nature," as quoted in Gary Wiener's The Environment in Henry David Thoreau's Walden, Greenhaven Press, 2010.

2. Thalif Deen, "U.S. Lifestyle Is Not Up for Negotiation," IPS, Inter Press Service News Agency, May 1, 2012, http://www.ipsnews.net/2012/05/us-lifestyle-is-not-up-for-negotiation/

3. Thomas Andrews, film character played by Victor Garber, "Titanic," Dir. James Cameron, 20th Century Fox/ Paramount Pictures, 1997, as quoted in imdb.com, http://www.imdb.com/character/ch0002351/quotes

4. Wikipedia.org, "Dodo," https://en.wikipedia.org/wiki/Dodo

July 6

1. C. JoyBell C., "C. JoyBell C.> Quotes> Quotable Quote," good-reads.com, https://www.goodreads.com/quotes/429964-some-people-say-they-will-not-believe-in-anything-they

2. Friedrich Nietzsche, "The Science of Joy" (also translated as "The Gay Science"), Section 125, Nietzsche's 1882 collection, Germany, as quoted in "God is Dead," wikipedia.org, https://en.wikipedia.org/wiki/God_is_dead

3. John Milton, "Book I," Paradise Lost, CreateSpace Independent Publishing, August 20, 2013, page 2.

4. C. JoyBell C., as quoted in quotesgem.pro, No. 119735, http://quotesgem.pro/author/c-joybell-c/17

5. C. JoyBell C., "C. JoyBell C.> Quotes> Quotable Quote," good-reads.com, https://www.goodreads.com/quotes/429964-some-people-say-they-will-not-believe-in-anything-they

July 13

1. Attributed to Voltaire, as quoted in brainyquote.com, http://www.brainyquote.com/quotes/quotes/v/voltaire163832.html

2. Attributed to Albert Einstein, as quoted in brainyquote.com, http://www.brainyquote.com/quotes/quotes/a/alberteins125368.html

July 20

1. David Abram, "Merleau-Ponty and the Voice of the Earth," wildethics.org, originally published in Environmental Ethics, volume 10 (1988), pp. 101-120, http://www.wildethics.org/essay/merleau-ponty-and-the-voice-of-the-earth/

2. Kathleen Miles, "Ray Kurzweil: In The 2030s, Nanobots In Our Brains Will Make Us 'Godlike,'" The WorldPost of The Huffington Post, October 1, 2015, http://www.huffingtonpost.com/entry/ray-kurzweil-nanobots-brain-godlike_560555a0e4b0af3706dbe1e2

3. Laura Sewall, as quoted in Knowledge Visualization and Visual Literacy in Science Education, edited by Anna Ursyn, IGI Global, Hershey, PA, 2016, page 193.

July 27

1. Rainer Maria Rilke, as quoted by Anita Barrows, "The Book of a Monastic Life, I.2.," Rilke's Book of Hours: Love Poems to God, Riverhead Books/Penquin, November 1, 2005.

2. Kathleen Miles, "Ray Kurzweil: In The 2030s, Nanobots In Our Brains Will Make Us 'Godlike,'" The WorldPost of The Huffington Post, October 1, 2015, http://www.huffingtonpost.com/entry/ray-kurzweil-nanobots-brain-godlike_560555a0e4b0af3706dbe1e2

3. Ibid.

August 3

1. Colin Murray Parks, referencing his work, as quoted in wikipedia.org, https://en.wikipedia.org/wiki/Colin_Murray_Parkes

2. Kathleen Miles, "Ray Kurzweil: In The 2030s, Nanobots In Our Brains Will Make Us 'Godlike,'" The WorldPost of The Huffington Post, October 1, 2015, http://www.huffingtonpost.com/entry/ray-kurzweil-nanobots-brain-godlike_560555a0e4b0af3706dbe1e2

3. Ibid.

4. Ibid.

5. Hans Christian Anderson, "The Emperor's New Clothes," Literary folktale, Fairy Tales Told for Children, First Collection, Third Booklet, published by C.A. Reitzel, Denmark, April 7, 1837.

August 10

1. World Council of Churches, meeting document in Granvollen, Norway in 1988, as quoted by ARC (Alliance of Religions and Conservation), arcworld.org, http://www.arcworld.org/faiths.asp?pageID=69

2. Kathleen Miles, "Ray Kurzweil: In The 2030s, Nanobots In Our Brains Will Make Us 'Godlike,'" The WorldPost of The Huffington Post, October 1, 2015, http://www.huffingtonpost.com/entry/ray-kurzweil-nanobots-brain-godlike_560555a0e4b0af3706dbe1e2

3. Ibid.

August 17

1. Carroll Quigley, referencing his work, as quoted in wikipedia.org, https://en.wikipedia.org/wiki/Carroll_Quigley

2. Rudyard Kipling, "The Ballad of East and West," as quoted in wikipedia.org, https://en.wikipedia.org/wiki/The_Ballad_of_East_and_West

3. The Flow Project presents, "Conscious Capitalism: Business success through social good." Radical Social Entrepreneurs, radicalsocialentreps.org, http://www.radicalsocialentreps.org/theory/conscious-capitalism/

4. Fred Kofman, Conscious Business: How to Build Value through Values, Sounds True publishing, Reprint edition, October 1, 2013, Prologue XXIII.

5. William Shakespeare, "The Merchant of Venice," 1596, as quoted in The Phrase Finder, phrases.org.uk, http://www.phrases.org.uk/meanings/390200.html

6. Hermes Trismegistus, "The Emerald Tablet of Hermes Trismegistus," as quoted in gnosticwarrior.com, http://gnosticwarrior.com/as-above-so-below.html

7. Attributed to Mahatma Gandhi, but actually a paraphrase summary of Gandhi's work by grandson Arun Ghandi, as quoted in Be Magazine, bemagazine.org, http://www.bemagazine.org/exclusive-origin-change-movement/

August 24

1. Dan Schawbel, "John Mackey: Why Companies Should Embrace Conscious Capitalism," Forbes Entrepreneurs, forbes.com, January 15, 2013, http://www.forbes.com/sites/danschawbel/2013/01/15/john-mackey-why-companies-should-embrace-conscious-capitalism/#328aaf656a3f

2. Layman P'ang as quoted by Jed McKenna, "Even the Poorest Thing Shines," Spiritual Enlightenment: The Damnedest Thing: Book One of The Enlightenment Trilogy, Wisefool Press, Nov. 25, 2009.

3. Fred Kofman, Conscious Business: How to Build Value through Values, Sounds True Publishing, 1st Edition, 2006, page 453.

August 31

1. Peter Matthies, "Welcome," Conscious Business Institute, consciousbusinessinstitute.com, http://www.consciousbusinessinstitute.com/indexReturn.html

2. Fred Kofman, Conscious Business: How to Build Value through Values, Sounds True publishing, Reprint edition, October 1, 2013, Prologue XXII.

September 7

1. Jeff King and Jeff Fromm, "Only Conscious Capitalists Will Survive," CMO Network/ forbes.com, Dec. 4, 2013, http://www.forbes.com/sites/onmarketing/2013/12/04/only-conscious-capitalists-will-survive/#7e1925d243bf

2. Ibid.

September 14

1. Richard Jefferies, "Gates of Another World," as quoted by Kim Taplin in Tongues in Trees: studies in literature and ecology, Green Books, First Edition, 1989, page 92.

2. Joni Mitchell, "Big Yellow Taxi," Ladies of the Canyon, Reprise label, March, 1970.

3. Robert Bly, The Kabir Book: Forty-Four of the Ecstatic Poems of Kabir, Bean Press, February 1, 1993.

FALL
Welcome to Fall

1. Attributed to Farid ud-Din Attar, "Rumi, Saadi, Hafiz (Poems and Quotes)," facebook.com,
https://www.facebook.com/RumiSaadiHafiz/?fref=nf

2. Marcel Proust, as quoted by Julia Kristeva, "The Captive," Time and Sense: Proust and the Experience of Literature, Columbia University Press, 1996, page vii.

3. Andre Gide, The Fruits of the Earth, Peter Pauper Press, First edition, 1969.

September 21

1. Lt. Col. Nicholson, film character played by Alex Guinness, "Bridge On the River Kwai," Dir. David Lean, Columbia Pictures, 1957, quoted by wikipedia.org,
https://en.wikipedia.org/wiki/The_Bridge_on_the_River_Kwai

September 28

1. Lynn Margulis from Stephen Harrod Buhner's Plant Intelligence and the Imaginal Realm: Beyond the Doors of Perception into the Dreaming of Earth, Bear & Company, 1st edition, May 3, 2014, page 101.

2. Cassandra L. Pinnick, Noretta Koertge, Robert F. Almeder, Scrutinizing Feminist Epistemology: An Examination of Gender in Science, Rutgers University Press, 2003, page 93.

October 5

1. Attributed to Guillaume Apollinaire, goodreads.com,
http://www.goodreads.com/quotes/17760-come-to-the-edge-he-said-we-can-t-we-re-afraid

2. Attributed to Shannon L. Alder, goodreads.com, http://www.goodreads.com/quotes/460061-fear-is-the-glue-that-keeps-you-stuck-faith-is

3. Attributed to John A. Shedd, 1928 collection of sayings, "Salt from My Attic," as quoted in quoteinvestigator.com, http://quoteinvestigator.com/2013/12/09/safe-harbor/

October 12

1. Christine Dell'Amore, "Species Extinction Happening 1,000 Times Faster Because of Humans?" nationalgeographic.com, http://news.nationalgeographic.com/news/2014/05/140529-conservation-science-animals-species-endangered-extinction/

October 19

1. John 13:34-35, New International Version (NIV) of The Bible, biblegateway.com, https://www.biblegateway.com/passage/?search=John+13%3A34-35

October 26

1. Thomas Lewis, Fari Amidi, Richard Lannon, A General Theory of Love, Reprint edition by Vintage publishers, January 9, 2001, page 228.

November 2

1. "Biomimicry 101," Biomimicry Institute, biomimicry.org, https://biomimicry.org/what-is-biomimicry/#.V4qxSaLakcM

November 9

1. Buckminster Fuller, "The Meaning of Wealth," Banker's Magazine, Vol. CCXIX, No. 1573, April, as quoted in Buckminster Fuller Institute, bfi.org, https://bfi.org/search?search_api_views_fulltext=wealth

November 23

1. Master Charles Cannon and Will Wilkinson, Forgiving the Unforgivable, 1st Edition, SelectBooks, February 21, 2012, page 104.

November 30

1. Henry Kimsey-House, Karen Kimsey-House, Phillip Sandahl, Laura Whitworth, Co-Active Coaching, Nicholas Brealey America, Third Edition, September 16, 2011, Introduction xvii.

December 7

1. Walt Whitman, Song of Myself, CreateSpace Independent Publishing Platform, September 24, 2012, page 3.

December 14

1. Stewart Brand, The Clock of the Long Now, Basic Books, Revised edition, April 6, 2000, page 2.

Fall Into Winter

1. Jalal-al-Din Rumi, as quoted by Nevit O. Ergin and Will Johnson, The Rubais of Rumi: Insane with Love, Inner Traditions/Bear & Co., July 17, 2007.

ABOUT THE AUTHOR

MASTER CHARLES CANNON is a modern spiritual teacher. He is a revered pioneer in the evolution of consciousness, known and respected as the founder of the Synchronicity Foundation for Modern Spirituality and the creator of High-Tech Meditation® and the Holistic Lifestyle™, which have empowered millions world-wide.

His previous books include *Forgiving the Unforgivable* which chronicles the true story of the survival of a small group of meditators demonstrating awakened living in the 2008 Mumbai terrorist attack and their forgiveness of the attackers thereafter. *Awakening from the American Dream* is a courageous presentation of spiritual remedies for 21st century social problems. His autobiography, *The Bliss of Freedom*, is a rare glimpse into the enlightening journey of a Western mystic in the modern world.

Comprehensive information about Master Charles Cannon and Synchronicity Foundation for Modern Spirituality can be explored at www.synchronicity.org.

ࢶ